Dad's **GREAT ADVICE®**
FOR
Parents of Teens

Other Dad's Great Advice Books available at greatadvicegroup.com

Dad's Great Advice for Teens

Dad's Great Advice: Top Ten Greatest Great Advice of All Time

Dad's Great Advice for College Students

Dad's Great Advice for Everyone

Dad's Great Advice for All Parents

Dad's Great Advice About Life Skills for Teens

Dad's GREAT ADVICE®

FOR Parents of Teens

MARC FIENBERG

Published in the United States by Story Press
info@greatadvicegroup.com
greatadvicegroup.com

Story Press, Dad's Great Advice, The Great Advice Group, and related
logos are trademarks of Story Press

Library of Congress Control Number: 2022943825

Paperback ISBN 978-1-7351804-4-1
Ebook ISBN 978-1-7351804-5-8
Hardcover ISBN 978-1-7351804-6-5

Printed in the United States of America

First Edition

For the best two parents of teens I've come across

in my extensive research: my own.

CONTENTS

BONUS GREAT ADVICE

Do You Really Need This Book?

This book is a concise summary of the twenty-five most important things that experts say every parent of a teenager should know.

Many parents of teenagers have everything under control—they never lose their temper, and always do the right thing when it comes to raising their teen. And by "many parents," I mean at least three or four parents in the world are doing everything right. Maybe even five. If you're one of those lucky parents who is doing it all perfectly, then you probably don't need to read any further.

But if you're not one of those perfect parents who has everything under control, if life with your teen seems a bit chaotic from time to time, then you might find it valuable to hear some Great Advice to help you parent your teen.

Just to be clear, this isn't Great Advice from just this one dad. Rather, it's the greatest of the Great Advice this dad has learned from speaking with and interviewing lots and lots of other dads, moms, therapists, psychologists, and parenting experts, as well as reading lots and lots of the best scientific parenting studies and research.

If you were to ask 1,000 people, "What's the most important advice you would give the parent of a teen?" this book contains the top twenty-five answers you'd get.

The Great Advice listed in this book will help you:

- Teach your teen how to make good decisions
- Help your teen improve their self-esteem
- Deal with your teen's dating life
- Teach your teen valuable life skills
- Stay sane and happy with a teen in your house
- Deal with bullying
- Help your teen deal with traumatic events
- Manage your teen's social media usage
- Deal with drugs and alcohol
- Get your teen to open up and connect with you
- Choose which battles to fight
- Find the right balance in your parenting
- Prepare your teen to live independently
- Develop a close relationship with your teen
- Appreciate your teen more

If you're looking for help in any of the areas above, then I'm confident that reading *Dad's Great Advice for Parents of Teens* will be well worth your time, and will help you become a better and happier parent.

Enjoy the book,

Marc

But Wait... There's More!

This book includes Great Advice specifically for parents of teens.

But over the many decades I've been collecting advice from people all over the world, I've come across lots of Great Advice that is great not only for parents of teens, but for everyone. And I've put the best of all of that Great Advice together all in one place.

This isn't just good advice. It's not just Great Advice. It's the crème de la crème of Great Advice! The Super Bowl of Great Advice! The best of the best Great Advice! It's...

The Top 10 Greatest Great Advice of All Time! (As recently voted on by our readers. And me.)

In appreciation of you purchasing this book, I'd like to give you *The Top 10 Greatest Great Advice of All Time* for free. To download it, just visit:

greatadvicegroup.com/top10advice6

REALIZE THAT YOU HAVE A NEW KID

You get a new kid every few years, so adapt as your child evolves and update your parenting strategies and how you interact with them.

It's probably a blur by now, but you might remember that, as an infant, your child was cute and cuddly and laughed at the funny faces you made. Ah, the good ol' days! And then something strange happened...

They got older.

And like a caterpillar that emerges as a beautiful butterfly, your child became a toddler, walking and talking, saying and doing cute things, and enjoying time reading with you. They kept getting older and older, metamorphosizing into a different kid every few years. Then recently, like a caterpillar that emerges as a rabid hyena, your child became a teenager.

If you think back over the years, you probably realize that your kid has changed a bit as time has passed. And by "changed a bit" I mean "they've become completely different people several times over." You probably stopped making funny faces at your kid long ago, once you realized that they no longer laughed when you did so, but instead responded with a simple "That's just weird." You probably stopped reading with your child long ago, once you realized that they'd rather just read by themselves. In many, many ways, over the length of your long, illustrious parenting career, you've already adjusted your parenting strategies and interactions with your child as they've moved from infant to toddler to school-aged child to pre-teen. And now that your kid is a teenager, you're going to have to do it again.

Except now, the stakes are higher, and the challenges harder.

Because the child who used to do what you asked of them simply because they respected you as a parent is now a teen who makes their own independent choices and needs to decide if what you asked makes sense to them. The child who used to participate in family activities to spend quality time with their parents is now a teen who wants to spend quality time with their friends. The child who used to follow the rules about doing homework right after school is now a teen who wants to set their own schedule and decide for themselves how much to prioritize schoolwork.

If parenting was a video game, the teenage years would be the boss battle. (Ask your teen if you don't know what a boss battle is. Or what a video game is.) All the skills you've learned up to this point are going to be required, plus a bunch of new skills that you've never had to develop. The sooner you realize this, the better. If your parenting strategy for your pre-teen is the same as for your teen, bad things lie ahead. If you're still assuming that you can just set some rules and expect that your teen is going to blindly follow them, you're in for a bit of a surprise. If you still believe you can simply increase the severity of punishments until total parenting domination is achieved, you're seriously underestimating the stubbornness level of a teenager.

It's time to mix it up. It's time to realize that the kid you've raised up to this point was a different human being than the one who stands before you today. It's time to adapt your mind-set and your strategies, and remember that what worked before, won't work anymore. It's time to shift from being an enforcer to becoming an advisor. It's time to treat your teen less like a child and more like a young adult. It's time to adapt from leading them to following their lead. It's time to give your teenager a bit more independence, responsibility, and freedom to screw up and learn some lessons on their own.

Be open-minded about how to update your parenting style and your relationship with your teenager, because they're more different now than they ever were before, and so you should treat them differently than you have before. If you succeed, you'll end up with a deeper connection with your child than you've ever experienced. And if you're less successful, you might have some very loud, angry, rough years ahead of you (in addition to spending a lot of time repairing all the damage!).

You get a new kid every few years, so adapt as your child evolves, and update your parenting strategies and how you interact with them.

"If parenthood came with a GPS, it would mostly just say... recalculating."

–Unknown

DAD'S GREAT ADVICE
FOR
PARENTS OF TEENS #2

TEACH THEM HOW TO
MAKE GOOD DECISIONS

Stop making decisions for your teen and move into the role of a trusted advisor who teaches them to think through their decisions in an organized, thoughtful way.

You may notice that a lot of Great Advice for parents of teens is centered on you giving more freedom and independence to your teen (with many important exceptions, of course). It's easy to take this advice and give your teen more freedom and independence if your teen is somewhat responsible and mature and rises to the challenge of their growing independence by making smart decisions.

But… let's face it. Not every teen is the epitome of responsibility. Not every teen makes good choices. In fact, as their parent, it might sometimes seem like your kid goes out of their way to intentionally try to beat the world record for the worst choice ever in the history of choices.

So what should you do if, instead of rising to the challenge of their growing independence, your teen takes advantage of their newfound independence and makes some bad choices? First, recognize that strict twenty-four-hour-a-day oversight of your teen isn't typically a winning strategy, especially not with a teen who is willing to sneak around and lie to gain their independence. As a result, you have to find the right balance between oversight and independence for your kid, which is not easy to do.

Regardless of where you find that balance between oversight and independence, there always will be, and should be, areas of your teen's life in which they are completely independent. And it's those areas in which your teen is independent that you have only one option when it comes to helping your child:

Teach your teen how to make good decisions.

I would apply the "easier said than done" label to that task, but even that might be a gross understatement. And yet, no matter how hard it is to teach your teen to make good decisions, it's one of those things that is so important to their development that us parents have to make every effort we can, at every opportunity we have, to do it. Whether your teen is now mature enough to start making good decisions, or whether they still need to grow a bit older and wiser before their better judgment kicks in, it's a skill they're going to eventually need to survive in this world of ours, so it's never too early to start trying to teach them.

The best time to teach a kid to make good decisions is one of those rare moments when they ask you for advice about something. Admittedly, for some teens, that moment may arrive about as often as a solar eclipse. Or perhaps less often. But when it does happen, jump on it.

When they ask you for your advice, don't immediately give them a straight answer. Tell them that it's a tough decision, you're torn, and you need more information before making a decision. And then share your thought process and ask them some follow-up questions based on a decision-making framework. If they can see the framework and strategy you use to help advise them on their decision, they can start to learn it and apply it themselves and start to make better decisions on their own.

Separately, you should take the time to actually teach them different decision-making frameworks, because they're probably not going to get taught that sort of thing in school. Although there are lots and lots of impressive decision-making frameworks out there to choose from, each designed by some really smart people and each dealing with different types of situations, we're dealing with teens here, so keep it simple. While there are many different types of situations in which your teen will have to make a difficult decision, focus on the two most common situations teens will find themselves in:

1. A situation where they have some time to choose between two or more options.

   EXAMPLES:
   - Which class should I take?
   - Which college should I go to?
   - Which party should I attend this weekend?

2. A more binary but urgent situation that deals with their health or safety.

   EXAMPLES:
   - Should I let that person drive me home?
   - Should I sneak into that movie theater?
   - Should I send this risqué photo of myself to that person?

The first type of situation is probably more common for most teens. For those times when they find themselves with some time to think before they have to choose between two or more options, teach your teen what I refer to as:

The Second-Easiest Decision-Making Framework for Teens

This is a simple methodology for teens to use when trying to choose between two options.

1. Define your decision options.

    EXAMPLE: Take the summer job as a lifeguard at the local pool with my friends, or as an intern at the architecture firm I aspire to work at full-time someday.

2. Define your goals that relate to the decision options in as much detail as possible, and prioritize each goal by importance.

    EXAMPLE: Make money, have fun with my friends, build toward my ultimate career goal, be outside in nature.

3. List the pros and cons of each decision option for each of the goals. Make sure you focus on both short-term and long-term consequences of each decision.

    EXAMPLE: The lifeguard job will let me be with my friends and be outside in nature, but it doesn't pay as well and doesn't work toward my ultimate goal of being an architect. The internship pays much better and works toward my career goal, but it's not with my friends and I'll be stuck indoors in an office all summer.

4. Weigh the pros and cons for each decision option across all the goals, giving extra weight to the most important goals, and choose the appropriate decision.

EXAMPLE: My most important goals are to be with my friends and make money, so even though I won't make as much money, I'm choosing the lifeguard job to be with my friends; OR my most important goals are to have fun with my friends and build toward my career, and because I'll still have a lot of time to hang out with my friends after work, I'm choosing the internship to build toward my career.

This is a very simple framework that your teen can use for many types of decisions, and it should give them the fundamental tools to help them make difficult decisions on their own. And yet, even this very simple framework might be too much for a teen to focus on, especially a teen who would much rather watch YouTube videos than think about their parent's boring decision-making framework. In the end, the good decisions your teen really needs to get right are those that fall into the second category: A more binary but urgent situation that deals with their health or safety. These are the decisions that will potentially do more to keep them out of real trouble.

For these types of decisions, disregard "The Second-Easiest Decision-Making Framework for Teens" and teach your kid "The Easiest Decision-Making Framework for Teens," which I like to call:

The Hospital Test

STEP 1:
Think about the worst possible consequences of your decision, and rule out any option for which the worst possible consequences involve a hospital, the police, or going viral on the internet for the wrong reasons.

That's all. It's that simple. Just one step. You can easily teach just one step to even the most unfocused, YouTube-distracted, teenage brain.

And while you're teaching your teen this one step, draw their attention to the fact that evaluating the probability of the worst possible consequence *actually happening* is not part of this process, primarily because teens think they're immortal and bulletproof and are notoriously poor at evaluating the right probability of something happening. Plus, it shouldn't really matter anyway, because if the worst possible consequences involve a hospital, the police, or going viral, even an infinitesimally small likelihood that it will happen is too much to risk.

Sum it up for your teen with this rule: When you're in a situation that can be described as "low probability but high impact," ignore the low probability and focus on the high impact.

The hospital test is especially valuable for the most important, potentially life-changing decisions of a teen's life. Those decisions that, for some reason, teens are notoriously awful at making. For example…

Trying to decide whether to be the first to dive off the quarry cliff into the water below? A hospital stay seems possible, so don't do it.

Trying to decide whether to steal that cool jacket off the rack because you can't afford it? Ending up handcuffed in the back of a police cruiser seems possible, so don't do it.

Trying to decide whether to text those revealing photos of yourself to the person you're dating? It's possible those photos could end up being posted online, so don't do it.

And of course, no piece of Great Advice about teaching your teens how to make good decisions would be complete without mentioning one of the most valuable decision-making tools in your teen's toolbox: Trusting their gut. Urge them to start getting in touch with their "gut feelings" and listening to what those feelings are telling them. (See *Dad's Great Advice for Teens #15*, "Don't Trust Your Brain to Make Decisions," in the bonus section of this book.)

When it comes down to it, your teen is going to have to start making a lot more decisions on their own as they get older. Prepare them now by teaching them how to evaluate their options with a simple framework. Stop making decisions for your teen and move into the role of a trusted advisor who teaches them to think through their decisions in an organized, thoughtful way.

"Children must be taught how to think, not what to think."

–Margaret Mead

DON'T LEAD THEM TOWARD A PARTICULAR CAREER

Convince your teen, and yourself, that the career choice that would make you most happy is the career choice that would make them most happy.

It might seem premature to start thinking about what career your teenager might end up in as an adult. And in fact, IT IS! And yet, I've seen more than my share of parents talking to their child about the benefits of being a doctor, or a dentist, or a "whatever," even as that child was still developing in the womb.

My good friend Archimedes Clutterbuck always encouraged his daughter, Cleopatra Clutterbuck, to be a lawyer. Sure enough, after four years of studying pre-law, and then another three years in law school, Cleo graduated at the top of her class, passed the bar, and was hired on to do corporate law at one of the most prestigious law firms in the country. To celebrate his daughter's success, Archimedes threw a huge party... which is where I was surprised to find him sulking in the corner. "She's been in therapy for months," he revealed, "and is dreading the idea of being a lawyer." Archie gave me a guilty look, knowing that his encouragement and insistence was the main reason Cleo spent seven years of her life pursuing a career that *he* was interested in, but *she* wasn't. He pushed her for years to follow his dream of success for his daughter, but in the end, knowing his daughter was unhappy with her future career made Archie sad as well. (Fortunately, Cleo never showed up for her first day of work at that law firm, and soon became a very happily employed nurse, with a very happy father.)

Most kids naturally want to make their parents happy and proud. Even if your teenager barely even speaks with you anymore, there's still a good chance that they secretly yearn for your approval. And if you make it clear over the years that you think they should one day become a lawyer, or a doctor, or an accountant, or any other career that you think they should have, there's a good chance that they'll take that into account when making their decision on what path to pursue. That will turn out to be fine if that really is the career that they naturally respond to. However, if it's not the career they're truly interested in, they may be in for a long road of unhappiness and depression ahead.

Chances are good that your teen will not head down the path you envision for them, and that's a good thing. Because if they do head down that path for you, and not for themselves, they'll likely be miserable.

Don't ever try to lead them down a path to a particular career, or even toward a particular interest or college major. Instead, encourage them to try new things, new interests and new hobbies. Pay close attention to what they respond to and what gets them excited. Once you figure out what that thing is, encourage your teen to jump into it with both feet. Or just one foot. Or even just a portion of a toe.

If your teen draws in their free time, encourage them to take drawing classes. If your teen loves gardening, give them their own plot of land in the backyard. If your teen loves to argue, encourage them to sign up for debate team. And sure, if your teen seems to be fascinated with how the human body works, you can certainly encourage them to learn more about the field of medicine.

However, never reveal to your teen which career you hope they choose. Better yet, never actually even have a career *you* hope they choose. Instead, help them figure out for themselves what career it is that *they* want to choose.

You can do that by helping your teen figure out what success means to them, not what success means to you. Help them find their type of success, not your type of success. (See *Dad's Great Advice for Everyone #1*, "Figure Out How to Be Successful," in the bonus section of this book.)

"But what if they want to take a really low-paying job?" you ask.

It's perfectly fine to make sure your teen knows the tradeoffs that come along with different career choices, including their potential future earnings, the hours they would need to work, their expected standard of living, the amount of schooling required, potential stress level, etc. And of course, if it's important to them that they have a lot of money, a prestigious career, and a big house, then by all means, encourage them to pursue a career that allows them to reach those goals.

But in this age of our enlightened youth, it's entirely possible that your teen will measure their success in a different way, like by how many people they help, or how many smiles they create, or how many races they win, or how many mouths they feed, or how many countries they visit, or how many refugees they find shelter for, or how much time they spend with their family. And if they can articulate why they're interested in the career they're interested in, are aware of any tradeoffs involved with that career, and are OK with those tradeoffs, then let them know that you're OK with it too.

Convince them, and yourself if necessary, that you don't care if they make a lot of money and have a prestigious career, just as long as they're happy.

Encourage them to pick a career that will inspire them and have them wanting to wake up in the morning to go to work. Remind them of the old saying by your good friend, Mark Twain:

"Find a job you enjoy doing, and you will never have to work a day in your life." And then remind them of the old saying by your other good friend, me: "Just because you share your parents' genes doesn't mean you share their dreams."

Ultimately, if you're like most parents, you'd rather have a happy child in a career you didn't choose for them, than an unhappy child in a career you did choose for them.

Convince your teen, and yourself, that the career choice that would make you most happy is the career choice that would make them most happy.

"*Just because my path is different doesn't mean I'm lost.*"

–Unknown

Dad's Great Advice
for
Parents of Teens #4

Give Them a
"Get Out of Jail Free Card"

Make sure that when your teen finds themselves in real trouble, you're the first person they call for help, not the last.

Imagine your child drove to a party that was miles away from home. They've promised you many times they wouldn't drink alcohol, and yet, despite their promises, they drank. And they're drunk. And the party is over. And they need to get home.

If your teen waits an hour for a taxi or Uber, they'll miss their curfew and get in trouble at home. If they call you to pick them up, they'll get in even more trouble because they're drunk. Their only chance of not getting in trouble is taking the risk of driving home. "I'm not that drunk," they tell themselves. And they're not driving on the highway, so they'll go slowly, and they'll be extra careful, and so they *probably* won't get pulled over, and it will *probably* be just fine, and then nobody will ever know that they were drunk, and nothing bad will happen. So they weigh the pros and cons of their decision, the risk of the small chance of a car accident versus the certainty of getting grounded for being drunk, and in the end, they decide that the best course of action is to…

Wait!

Before your teen makes that decision, if you had the opportunity to influence them to decide not to drive home drunk, would you take it? If you could somehow make it easier on them to make the right decision, wouldn't you want to do that?

That's what a "Get Out of Jail Free Card" does for your teen. A "Get Out of Jail Free Card" is a promise you make to them that goes something like this:

"I want you to make smart choices in life. But from time to time, if you're anything like me, you will make some not-so-smart choices. And you'll get in over your head, and you'll find yourself not just in a bad situation, but a really bad situation. When you do find yourself in that bad situation, you'll probably wish you had somebody to help you out, especially your parent. And yet, despite how bad the situation is, and how much you really need help, you might feel too embarrassed or afraid of getting in trouble to ask for that help from me. But my primary job as your parent is to keep you safe, not to punish you or teach you a lesson. So I promise you this: If you ever are in a position where you really need some help, especially if your safety is in question, but you're too embarrassed or afraid to ask for it, call me. I'll be there for you. And after I get there and help you out of that situation, I promise you that you can use this "Get Out of Jail Free Card" with me, which says that I won't punish you, I won't hold it against you, and I won't even ask you what happened. Once you're back home, safe and sound, we will act like it never happened. And one day, thirty years from now, when you're a parent yourself, if you want to finally share the story with me, then we'll have a good laugh about it, but otherwise, we'll act like it never happened."

And if you want to put your "Get Out of Jail Free Card" on steroids, choose a close adult friend you trust and let your teen know that, if they really don't want to call you, they can call your friend, and you've instructed that friend to come to your child's rescue and honor the "Get Out of Jail Free Card" by never, ever letting you know that they did it.

Now the hardest aspect of this whole thing is that, if your kid someday really does use your "Get Out of Jail Free Card," you've got to make sure you keep up your end of the bargain and don't ask them any questions, no matter how strong the urge.

Is it hard not to know what's going on with your kid, especially when you know they've gotten themselves into a bit of trouble? Yes! But keeping them safe comes first and foremost. And without giving them the safe, consequence-free option that the "Get Out of Jail Free Card" gives them in the first place, whatever trouble they're in is likely to turn from bad to worse before you ever have the chance to find out about it and help them.

Plus, even though you're making a promise not to ask them what happened, you already know the most important information: they got in over their head. And knowing that allows you to keep a closer eye on them in the future and perhaps find a way to help them in a different manner.

A "Get Out of Jail Free Card" is your best chance to do everything you can to prevent a bad situation from getting worse. Give your child a "Get Out of Jail Free Card" and make sure that when they find themselves in real trouble, you're the first person they call for help, not the last.

"Keeping the big picture in mind is one of the most important things parents can do, and also one of the hardest."

–T. Berry Brazelton

DAD'S GREAT ADVICE
FOR
PARENTS OF TEENS #5

HELP THEM WITH THEIR
SELF-ESTEEM

Healthy self-esteem is one of the most important qualities for your teen to have, so keep a constant eye on it and take every opportunity to do whatever you can to improve it.

If there was a list of the top qualities you'd want your teenage child to have, it would probably include: a deep and undying respect for their parents, the insatiable urge to clean up the house and cook gourmet meals for the family, and the ability to have a calm, rational discussion and selflessly admit when they may have held the wrong opinion about something. Yet, while all of these qualities are nice, there's one quality in particular that rises to the very top of the list…

Self-esteem.

The term "self-esteem" is often used interchangeably with "confidence," although they're slightly different concepts. In short, self-esteem refers to whether you feel good about yourself, and if you feel worthy enough to deserve happiness and love. Confidence is about believing in yourself and your abilities. Confidence can and often does improve self-esteem, but it's possible for somebody to have confidence in themselves or their skills while still not having high self-esteem.

Lots of kids grow up with an abundance of self-esteem when they're toddlers or younger kids. But then sadly, at some point around their teenage years, that healthy sense of self-esteem often takes a hit. It can be chipped away slowly over time by social media influences, or in an instant by a bully at school, but once it takes a hit, a teen's self-esteem can easily get worse and worse.

And that's a shame, because a teen's self-esteem is amazingly important in setting them up to be successful, act independently, try new things, and take healthy risks, among many other positive behaviors. Teens with low self-esteem feel bad about themselves, are too hard on themselves, and believe they're not good enough. These feelings can become a self-fulfilling prophecy, and can create a downward spiral of other problems that build off of each other, such as falling in with troublemaking friends, struggling to have healthy relationships, battling anxiety or depression, having poor body image, engaging in early sexual activity, and developing alcohol or drug problems.

If your teen has the occasional moments of low self-esteem, there are several things you can do as a parent to help snap them out of it or, better yet, build the skills that will keep their self-esteem high in the first place.

First, it's important to recognize that your teen's self-esteem has several drivers. One of the biggest drivers is your teen's own confidence in their abilities. When they become proficient at some hobby or sport or skill, especially when they become better at it than many of their peers, it naturally improves their self-esteem. Your teen's mindset is a major driver as well. We all live in our own heads all day long, but your teen's "inner voice" can be particularly irrational and overly critical, resulting in them constantly talking down to themselves and creating a downward spiral of negative thoughts. And of course, one of the biggest drivers of their self-esteem can be how their friends treat them (surprise, surprise).

But all those self-esteem drivers might be eclipsed by one other important driver: you! Their parent.

That's right. Despite the fact that they might ignore you, call you names, and say that they don't give a damn what you think, they secretly actually do give a damn what you think. And even if you've got one of those teens who genuinely doesn't give a damn what you think, you can still do lots of things to have a positive impact on their self-esteem and confidence.

One of the more straightforward things you can do to help their self-esteem is to figure out what some of their strengths and passions are, and encourage your teen to spend more time developing them. If they really enjoy chess, encourage them to join the chess team. If they're great at arguing with you, encourage them to join the debate team. If they're fantastic spellers, encourage them to compete in a spelling bee. It doesn't really matter what activity they focus on; if they feel like they excel in that activity or just really enjoy that activity, and spend a lot of time doing it, it's certainly going to help their self-esteem.

Separate from that, you can help their self-esteem by encouraging them to have good friends who treat them well, and subtly steer them away from friends who are toxic. "Subtly steer" are the operative words here. Be careful never to come right out and tell your teen that you don't like one of their friends. Doing so inevitably backfires and is likely to cause your teen to hang out with the problem friend even more, just to assert their independence. There's nothing more exciting to a teen than having a friend their parent doesn't approve of!

Instead, when they want to make plans with one of their friends that treats them well, facilitate those plans as much as possible by driving them wherever and whenever they need to be driven, and offer to pay for any activities they plan together. Conversely, it's totally OK to be "busy with work" when your teen needs a ride to hang out with one of their friends who doesn't treat them well, or to come up with an excuse not to pay for the activities with one of those same friends.

And while you never want to say that their friend is "bad," it's certainly OK to offer your opinions on that friend's behavior. For example, when your teen's friend does something thoughtless, instead of saying, "I really don't like that friend of yours," try saying "I really like your friend, but don't you think that was a total jerk move they made?" Draw their attention to the friend's actions, rather than their overall character, which your teen can eventually draw their own conclusions about.

In an extreme example, where one of their "friends" or somebody else is outright bullying them, it pays to take a much more active role and get involved more directly. You have to adjust your tactics to the severity of the specific situation, but if your teen is being bullied and doesn't have the ability to handle it themselves, don't be afraid to take quick, big, definitive steps to get involved and put an end to it, whether that means involving the authorities at their school, speaking directly to the parents of the bully, or even getting law enforcement involved. Bullying can be devastating to a teenager and have long-lasting effects, so make sure if it crops up that you treat it seriously and decisively.

Another thing to help your teen with is trying to keep a positive attitude. If you're the type of parent that asks your kids not to curse in the house, next time your teen says something negative about themselves, treat it like a curse word. When they say, "I can't do that, I'm not smart enough," you reply as if they just dropped an F-bomb, with "Please do not talk like that in my house. You know I don't like it when you use that language." If you discourage your teen from insulting other kids in your house (and you should), you should also discourage your teen from insulting themselves in your house.

Another good strategy for increasing self-esteem in your teen is to help them set goals for themselves and work toward them. Try to have a discussion with your teen to help identify some short-term and long-term goals that are achievable. Then help them break down those goals into smaller tasks and set a schedule for achieving those tasks. You don't want to force them to work toward those goals, because then they feel absolutely no ownership in achieving them, but you do want to encourage and motivate them in any way you can. A simple, "Do you need any help keeping on track with your schedule?" will suffice. (See *Dad's Great Advice About Life Skills for Teens #7*, "Set Formal Goals," in the bonus section of this book.)

One of the easier ways of increasing your teen's self-esteem is to get them to do some sort of community service. And by "get them to do it" what I really mean is "make them do it." While it's hard to motivate some teens to do anything that doesn't involve their phone, this is important enough that it's a battle worth fighting. It's important because helping others has been scientifically proven to be one of the key drivers of happiness and gratitude, and it can give your teen a sense of purpose, which in turn leads to higher self-esteem. Ask your teen to find a community service activity that appeals to them, whether it's delivering meals to the hungry, volunteering at an animal shelter, or just picking up trash off the street on the way home from school.

And of course, remember that helping your teen with their self-esteem doesn't just revolve around improving their self-esteem directly. It's also important to help them deal with and manage their disappointments, so that those disappointments don't lead to huge hits to their self-esteem. You can help them by listening and empathizing when they experience a disappointment, encouraging them to use constructive coping mechanisms to deal with it (like playing sports or going for a walk, rather than drinking or drugs), and helping them to keep some perspective about it and to problem-solve to avoid the same situation again.

Connected to this is trying to help your teen focus on the positive things in their life that are within their control, rather than obsessing over bad stuff that has already happened that they can't control. You have to strike the right balance here, because if you're always looking for the silver lining in everything, even stuff that really doesn't have many positive aspects to it, you'll start to come off as insincere or unreliable, and they'll come to expect a false sense of positivity from you. It's more about acknowledging that the bad stuff is bad, not overreacting to it or focusing on it, and quickly moving on to things that are still within their control. For example, if they come home with a bad grade on a test, give a quick, "That sucks that you didn't do well," and then move on to, "What areas do you think you can work on to prepare for the next test?"

There are lots of things you can do as a parent to help your child improve if their self-esteem takes a dip every now and then. However, for some teens, self-esteem can take more than a dip—it can drop into a deep valley and threaten to stay there. If this sounds like your teen, then my Great Advice to you is even more succinct and simple than everything mentioned earlier:

Get help from a professional therapist.

There are entire books written on improving self-esteem and confidence in children, but it's such an important issue that, if it's a real problem that affects your teen on regular basis, you shouldn't try to help your teen on your own. Low self-esteem is one of the most common things that therapists work with teens on, so you'll probably find that, no matter how much outside research you do, you'll still be outgunned by a professional who has worked with teens for years on this issue. So if your teen is already well down the low self-esteem road, don't try to fix it on your own. Call in the professionals.

Healthy self-esteem is one of the most important qualities for a teen to have, so keep a constant eye on it and take every opportunity to do whatever you can to improve it.

"Behind every child who believes in himself is a parent who believed first."

–Unknown

PUT YOUR OWN OXYGEN MASK ON FIRST

If you don't take care of yourself, you'll have a hard time taking care of your teen.

All the parenting advice out there and in this book is focused around your child. Which obviously makes a lot of sense. And if you're the kind of person who wants to spend your free time reading advice on how to be a better parent, rather than, oh, I don't know, absolutely ANYTHING else, then you're probably the type of parent who doesn't mind focusing a lot of your energy on your child instead of yourself. That's all good. But sometimes...

You gotta look out for number one. (You are the number one I'm referring to here, not your teen, in case that wasn't clear.)

If you've been on a commercial airliner and paid attention to the flight attendant's safety announcement, as I'm sure we ALL do in order to learn how to use the very complicated seatbelt, then you've probably heard this Great Advice before: "If there should be a change in cabin pressure, put your own oxygen mask on first before assisting others." If you try to help somebody else with their mask but lose consciousness before you get the chance to finish, you're no help to anybody, and have just become a person who somebody else now needs to help. Putting your own oxygen mask on first has become a cliché, but it still makes sense.

Treat your house like a turbulent airliner that just lost cabin pressure at 30,000 feet, (which is what many households with a teenager in them actually do feel like) and do the equivalent of putting your own oxygen mask on first by taking some time out of your day to put yourself first. Aside from the fact that you deserve it because you're a parent who has raised a human being for more than a decade, putting yourself first for a while keeps you relaxed, patient, diplomatic, positive, present, and sane. And those are pretty important qualities for any parent to have, but *especially* the parent of a teenager. After all, no matter how much you care about your teenager, you won't be able to help them effectively if you need help yourself. Plus, taking the time to invest in your own well-being and recharge your batteries is a great quality to model for your teen, because it's probably something that a lot of teens could do better at themselves.

If you've got the time (and especially if you don't have the time), take sixty minutes a day for your "Me Hour." It can be an hour doing absolutely anything you want, as long as it's something that recharges your batteries. Some ideas: exercising, reading, walking, hiking, meditating, taking a bath, biking, painting, listening to music, gardening, cooking, or even napping.

Block your Me Hour off on your calendar each day (and weekends too!) so nobody tries to steal it away from you. While you're welcome to schedule it any time you'd like, I highly recommend you start your day with your Me Hour, even if it means waking up an hour earlier. Why? Because as we all know, other things and other people (particularly teens) have the tendency to impose themselves on your schedule, even when you block time off on your calendar, and before you know it, the day flies by and you never manage to get your Me Hour in.

When that hour comes along each day, treat that appointment like you would any other appointment on your calendar—honor it! Don't cancel the meeting with yourself unless a true emergency comes up—and remember that true emergencies don't come up very often. A true emergency is "My kid broke their arm." A true emergency is not "I need to pick up the jacket my teen forgot at cousin Emma's house, which is an hour away," and it's definitely not "My boss needs me to prepare a cover sheet for the TPS reports for the Weekly Estimated Net Usage Statistics meeting."

If you're one of those people who is going to feel guilty about prioritizing a little self-care every day, just remind yourself that one hour of your day represents 4.2% of your time. It's not selfish to spend less than 5% of your day on yourself, especially when you're giving 33% of your time to your job, 33% to sleep, and almost 30% to your teen and everybody else that needs you. Let's be honest, 4.2% isn't too much to ask, so prioritize it. Treat it like a meeting on your calendar, and make that hour sacred.

Taking a Me Hour each day is one of the easiest ways to become a better parent. "Do it for the kids," and make sure you spend at least one hour a day recharging your batteries by doing something that helps numero uno (that's you). Because if you don't take care of yourself, you'll have a hard time taking care of your teen.

"To be a good parent, you need to take care of yourself so that you can have the physical and emotional energy to take care of your family."

–Michelle Obama

GET THEM READY TO LEAVE YOU

Your ultimate goal is to raise independent human beings capable of surviving and thriving on their own, so give them some independence now and see what they do with it.

Many years ago, when your child was much younger, they depended on you for their very survival. They depended on you feeding them, giving them water, keeping them warm at night, and, most importantly, wiping their butt. And over the years, much of your job as a parent was to slowly but surely teach them all the skills they will need to be ready to leave the nest one day.

But now, years later, things may be a bit different. Depending on exactly how far into the teenage years your kid is, you're probably realizing that they're a bit less dependent on you than they used to be. You might have two possible reactions to that. One reaction is that you realize that your child doesn't need you as much, and as a result, you get a bit sad and depressed. Another reaction is that you realize that your child doesn't need you as much, and as a result, you break out into song and dance and party like it's 1999. Or maybe you even feel a bit of both at the same time.

There's one camp that consists of parents who are dreading the day their kid leaves home, and there's another camp of parents who are counting the days until their kid leaves home.

Regardless of which camp you're in, if your teens are like most, once they reach the ripe old age of eighteen, they will indeed leave home, whether you like it or not. And since that's inevitable, it makes sense to prepare them for it as much as possible, regardless of how you happen to feel about it.

Preparing them to be independent adults living on their own outside of your house often means giving them as much autonomy as they can handle before leaving. That means trying to become less and less of a parent and only stepping in in cases where they're about to make a huge, impactful, and significant mistake. (See *Dad's Great Advice for Parents of Teens #21*, "Let Them Make Stupid Mistakes," in this book.)

It only makes sense. The more autonomy you can give them while they still live under your roof, the more opportunity you have to work through any issues or hurdles they might encounter while you're still around to help.

If your child is in their early teen years, then congratulations, you still have quite a bit of time before having to worry about all this. But if your kid is sixteen or seventeen, it's time to start thinking about throwing some responsibility, freedom, and autonomy their way, just to see how they handle it... maybe even some responsibility, freedom, and autonomy that you're not yet fully comfortable handing over.

Where and when to give them some of that independence is a tricky balancing act, primarily because your teen is on the border between being an immature child who needs guidance, boundaries, and rules, and an independent, responsible adult who can make good decisions on their own. You have to learn to juggle when to treat them like a child and step in and help them, and when to treat them like an adult and step back and allow them to manage their own life.

Regardless of where you define that border, as they approach the day they leave home, make sure you're handing more and more responsibility over to them, but only with the agreement that they handle that responsibility... responsibly. For instance, you might want to push their curfew back a bit each year, provided they make it home on time each time they go out. You might want to not keep such a close eye on their schoolwork, provided they keep their grades up. Those are some of the easy issues. The tougher issues you have to deal with are how much autonomy to give them regarding more "adult" issues like drinking, smoking, vaping, drugs, and sex.

You might decide to be fairly strict with your teens and forbid them from any drinking, or drugs, or sexual activity until they're older. Whether that's a good idea or not, you have to decide for yourself. However, I most certainly can tell you that, at some point, a teen who wants to drink, smoke, vape, do drugs, or have sex is going to do those things—with or without your permission—while they're living at home with you, or once they leave home. And once you come to terms with that, you have to decide whether you think it's better that they do all that "adult" stuff for the first time when they're on their own, away from home, or that they do it a year or two earlier while they're at home and you're able to help them through it if they allow things to get out of control.

While I certainly wouldn't advise you to encourage or push your teenager to try drinking, smoking, vaping, or drugs, or have sex if they're not expressing interest, if your older teen is asking you about it, I would be realistic about how many real options you have when it comes to stopping them (not many, actually), and realistic about the benefits that might come with being able to closely monitor their actions during a critical time.

If you do decide to allow them to try some adult vices, I would do my best to get them to agree to do so responsibly, and according to the rules you agree upon with them. For example, if your kid starts drinking alcohol, here's a set of rules you can use to help make sure that they always keep their drinking under control (these rules work great for vaping, smoking, and other vices as well):

- Don't drink more than twice a month.
- Only drink on Friday or Saturday nights, never during the day.
- Don't drink to excess.
- If you do drink to excess and throw up, don't drink again for a month.
- If you have even one sip of alcohol, don't drive. (It's not worth trying to figure out if you're impaired.)
- If your driver has even one sip of alcohol, don't get in a car with them.
- If you set these (or similar) rules for yourself and consistently break them, ask for help.
- If you get drunk once a week or more, ask for help.
- If your friends say they're worried about your drinking, ask for help.

Separately, if your teen expresses interest in becoming sexually active, the list of rules is a bit shorter, but just as important.

- Always use a condom. Every time. All the time. No exceptions.

And whether your teen has expressed interest in becoming sexually active or not, before they leave the house, it's a good idea to make sure you have a frank discussion with them about sexual issues, in preparation for a time in the future when they do become active. That's right. It's time for… "The Talk!" Important topics you should cover in the discussion include Sexually Transmitted

Infections (STIs), what consent means, how to practice safe sex, healthy versus unhealthy or abusive relationships, masturbation, and porn. Additionally, if you're the parent of a teen female, it's a good idea to make sure they're set up with some sort of birth control before they leave the house. (And for the record, there's absolutely no evidence that discussing sexual topics with your teen or putting your daughter on birth control will cause them to become sexually active any sooner than they would've otherwise, so don't use that as an excuse to avoid some uncomfortable discussions with your teen.)

Ultimately, remind yourself that your teenager will soon be on their own, and the better you prepare them for life on their own, the better off your kid will be over the long term. Your ultimate goal is to raise independent human beings capable of surviving and thriving on their own, so give them some independence now and see what they do with it.

"The greatest gifts you can give your children are the roots of responsibility and the wings of independence."

–Denis Waitley

THEY WILL DO AS YOU DO, NOT AS YOU SAY

Don't just talk the talk, but walk the walk by actually modeling the behavior yourself that you'd like to instill in your teenager.

When my good friend Archimedes Clutterbuck was a teenager, he and his three siblings would visit his grandparents every now and then, and as you might expect, the siblings would spend a lot of time yelling at and bickering with each other. His grandfather, Old Man Clutterbuck, didn't take too kindly to all the arguing and noise, and so he'd constantly try to teach Archie and his siblings, "You can get your point across diplomatically, without yelling at each other." And for a while, it would work.

Hours later though, Archie would catch his grandfather yelling at and bickering with his grandmother, and, with a devious grin on his face, he'd tell his grandfather, "You can get your point across diplomatically, without yelling at each other." His grandfather's answer was always the same: "Do as I say, not as I do."

That advice actually might work well for a few months with very young kids, who do what they're told simply to make their parents happy and avoid a "time out" or a stern look of disapproval, but that stage doesn't last very long. Eventually, kids hit the age where getting a "time out" doesn't faze them, and a stern look of disapproval from their parent starts to elicit nothing but laughter.

Years ago, scientists discovered something they call Social Learning Theory, which is the gold standard when it comes to complicated, self-important scientific terms used to describe something amazingly simple and intuitive. In this case, Social Learning Theory is the name given to the idea that people learn from watching others. I know… not exactly rocket science, right? If you haven't figured out by now that your kids watch everything you do and act out the same behaviors they see, then you haven't been paying attention.

And by the time kids hit their teen years, they're definitely on to us for our parental hypocrisies. You can't tell your teenager to use social media less and then spend three hours scrolling on Facebook. You can't tell your teenager to always tell the truth and then enlist their cooperation to get the youth discount by saying they're only twelve years old instead of thirteen. And you can't teach your child not to smoke and then sneak a cigarette out on the porch after they go to sleep. Because your teenager will catch you. I promise you, that clever teen will catch you.

You might naturally be wondering, "How the heck can I model good behavior for my teenager without all the hard work and sacrifice of doing the good behavior myself? How can I get them to do as I say, not as I do?" Well, I've got some bad news for you…

You can't.

There is no shortcut. Teenagers aren't dumb. If you teach them to do one thing, and they see you doing another thing, whatever thing you taught them flies out the window and the thing you did is the new (lower) bar that's been set for them. If it's OK for their parent to do, it's OK for them to do.

So while there is unfortunately no way around this sad fact, you can rejoice in the knowledge that there is one nice side effect of trying to model good behavior for your kids: it will inspire you to raise your game. A lot.

When my good friend Archimedes got older and had kids of his own, his grandfather's "Do as I say, not as I do" came back to haunt him. Archie is, for the most part, a kind and considerate person. Over the years, he stressed to his kids the importance of being kind and considerate to others. And fortunately, his kids grew up to be exceptionally kind and considerate young people. However, there's an interesting dynamic in Archie's house. Even though Archie is generally kind and considerate to people as well, he's got a huge Achilles heel: customer service representatives. When he's on the phone with a customer service representative, particularly a rep from one of those companies with a notoriously poor customer service reputation, like the cable company, the phone company, or an airline, he sometimes loses it. And by using the phrase "loses it," I'm being generous.

Eventually, when he starts yelling at the top of his lungs at the customer service representative to get his internet connection working again, his teens hear him. But they don't *just* hear him— they come in the room to listen up close. They intentionally force his hand, making him stare straight into the eyes of the very children he raised to be kind and considerate people, while he himself behaves like the opposite of a kind and considerate person. Rather than send one message to his kids and display another different one, he decides to raise his game. Now, he's a lot more civil to customer service representatives (although he still has slow internet).

Start with the easy ones. If you tell your teen not to use their phone at the dinner table, make sure you put your phone away too. If you tell your teen to make sure they say "please" and "thank you," make sure you're being just as polite. If you tell your teen to remember to do their chores, make sure you're taking care of your chores and responsibilities too.

It isn't easy to move from merely teaching good behaviors to your teen to actually modeling good behaviors for them. You'll most certainly make mistakes and exhibit some behavior that's completely hypocritical and at odds with what you teach your teen. But the good news is that, in doing so, you'll be able to model a different (but just as important) behavior in the process: the ability to admit when you're wrong and show that even you're not perfect.

Give up your "do as I say, not as I do" outlook. Don't just talk the talk, but walk the walk by actually modeling the behavior yourself that you'd like to instill in your teenager.

"Your children will become what you are, so be what you want them to be."

–Unknown

GET THEM INVOLVED
IN AN ACTIVITY

Actively participating in an extracurricular activity could be the single most important thing your teen can do to more easily navigate their remaining teen years.

"I'm bored."

The average teen utters this statement to their parents approximately 3.4 million times by the time they're eighteen. Or maybe that's just the number of times it feels like your teen utters this statement—I forget. Regardless, kids get bored.

When toddlers get bored, they just yank on your shirt a couple hundred times until you play a game with them. But when teens get bored, it gets a bit more serious. Bored teens have Instagram, Snapchat, Netflix, TikTok, and a bunch of other mind-numbing apps to occupy their time. However, even teens get bored of their phones every now and then, and that's when they look for other things to do.

Unfortunately, the "other things" they look to do don't typically include healthy, productive activities like starting their own business, making jewelry, cooking, helping around the house, or achieving world peace. Instead, bored kids sometimes look to cure their boredom in other, less ideal ways, such as drinking, smoking, drugs, joining a gang, shoplifting, or just simply causing trouble. If only there were a place where teens don't get bored. Fortunately, there is! It's called...

Iceland.

In Iceland, the government has made boredom illegal. Well, maybe not illegal, but they certainly have put a dent in teenage boredom. Two decades ago, Icelandic teens were among the heaviest drinkers in Europe, so the government stepped in and put a bunch of interventions into place. One of the most significant things they did was to pay for teens to partake in extracurricular activities, from sports, orchestra, and dance, to yoga, chess, and singing. And if there's one thing teens really like, it's getting stuff for free. So teens signed up for extracurricular activities in droves. And as it turns out, the busier teens became due to their extracurricular activities, the less free time they had to spend on all the unsavory byproducts that result from boredom, which led to some pretty amazing results: Drinking, smoking, and drug use among teens in Iceland dropped from the highest in Europe to the lowest in Europe.

Bored teens crave excitement and the "high" they get from that excitement. As it turns out, they're able to get that "high" they crave not just from drugs and alcohol, but also from participating in an activity that they're passionate about. Teens that participate in activities essentially get high on their own brain chemistry!

However, teens getting excited by activities and being more likely to avoid drugs and alcohol aren't the only benefits. Teens that participate in extracurricular activities and hobbies are also more likely to stay in high school, get higher grades, build friendships, feel independent, form a sense of belonging, have higher confidence and self-esteem, and manage their time better. Oh, and did I mention that it gives your teen something to write about when it comes to applying to college? Not bad, eh?

The big question still looming though is, how can you get your teen involved in extracurricular activities?

Well, it certainly ain't easy, but there's always a way. Focus on your teen's past and current hobbies and interests and pursue the ones that are most easily transferrable into a formal extracurricular activity. For instance, if your teen is into soccer, it's pretty easy to find a soccer league to join in most communities, and many leagues are inexpensive, if not free. On the other hand, if your teen's favorite activity is a bit more obscure, like needlepoint or archery, it might be a little more difficult to match them up with other teens in a formal extracurricular activity. At that point, you can either look for a different activity your teen is interested in that's already established in your area, or you could always try to create a formalized activity yourself, simply by finding other teens that share the interest. Sure, it takes a lot more effort, but you never know—there just might be enough teens in your area to start that needlepoint club and train for the next national needlepoint competition.

Regardless, the writing is on the wall. Do whatever it takes to encourage your teen to find a sport, hobby, job, or activity they're passionate about and jump in with both feet. Pay for it. Drive them to it. Help them start it or find others to join them. Watch them practice. Help them practice. Attend their competitions or performances. Brag to your friends about their amazing talent and skill.

Actively participating in an extracurricular activity could be the single most important thing your teen can do to more easily navigate their remaining teen years.

"*Keep busy at something. A busy person never has time to be unhappy.*"

–Robert Louis Stevenson

BECOME A CONVERSATIONAL NINJA

Even if your teen has no interest in talking to their parents, you owe it to them to strategize in every way possible to make it as easy to talk to you as you can.

Over the course of history, mankind has accomplished some pretty amazing things. We've launched human beings 238,000 miles into space to walk on the moon. We've quickly created vaccines to slow the spread of a terrible virus spreading across the world. And perhaps most notably, we've even been able to create a phone app that allows us to film ourselves doing silly dances to instantly share with the entire world (it's called TikTok; ask your teen.) However, even after all these amazing accomplishments, we've still not yet managed to crack one of the most perplexing problems that has faced parents for thousands of years: how to get our teenagers to talk to us.

Enough already. That ends now.

First, you need to recognize how important it is to solve this problem. Keeping the lines of communication open with your teenager is imperative if you want to have any chance of knowing when issues or problems come up in their life (or even when great things are going on in their life). Otherwise, teens have been known to keep all their problems bottled up inside them, not sharing them with you, with friends, or with anybody, until those problems get way out of control. Obviously, that's not ideal. You want to be there to help your teen with their issues, and you want to catch those issues as early as possible.

Second, it's important to know that it's not your fault. It appears as though the teenage human brain is just naturally wired to shut down most communication with the two people who created that brain about thirteen years after they created it. It seems to be encoded in their DNA, in a gene that scientists have named the "I-have-nothing-to-say-to-those-people-who-helped-me-survive-this-long gene." Thankfully, that gene only remains active for about a decade (or until that brain realizes it needs help paying for college).

Luckily though, there are things you can do to that stubborn teenaged brain to increase your chances of breaking down its defenses and reestablishing communication with it from time to time, at least temporarily. But those things aren't obvious or easy to do. It takes strategy, cunning, and training. You need to become... a conversational ninja.

Your training begins now.

One of the most important things to remember when trying to get a teenaged brain (and the actual teenager that brain resides in) to talk to you is that timing is everything. Choose times and places where you're not competing with lots of other distractions. The dinner table, shopping, or downtime while on vacation could all be good options.

Make sure you remember this key trick: create side-by-side situations where you can't easily make eye contact with your teen. The more difficult the discussion, the more a teenager hates making eye contact, so take some pressure off them by sitting side-by-side, instead of across from them. For instance, sitting side-by-side at a restaurant counter is a great place to encourage conversation. Other great situations for no-eye-contact discussions are going for a walk or a hike, shooting baskets on a basketball court, walking the dog, or playing miniature golf. Extra credit for creating a side-by-side situation where you've got a relatively captive audience, like in a car, or on a ski lift.

Even better, try talking to them late at night, once you've turned the lights down. Not only is it darker (less eye contact), but there's nothing like exhaustion to help lower a teen's guard.

Make sure the questions you ask them are open-ended questions, rather than yes/no questions. "How do you feel about that?" is better than "Does that make you feel bad?" Similarly, "What happened after that?" is better than "Did you confront them after that?"

Open-ended questions are great, but remember that you also don't want to come off as a detective. You don't want to ask a million probing questions. You don't need perfect insight into every last detail about what they're saying. You don't want to make them feel like they're being interrogated. Look for the right balance—ask enough questions to understand the situation, but not so many that your teen gets exasperated. Try to read the room.

Another thing you can do to help get your teen talking more is to show your own vulnerability, which will give your teen more comfort in reciprocating with their own vulnerability. One way to do that is by sharing your own problems, mistakes, and feelings with them. (See *Dad's Great Advice for Parents of Teens #13*, "Share Your Problems with Them," in this book.) Obviously, we don't want to burden our children with serious issues, but it's perfectly OK to share along the lines of, "Boy, did I have a terrible day at work, let me tell you about it," or even "I have a problem that I'm working through that I want to get your opinion on."

Also, try sharing stories with them about when you were a teen and the problems you had. Telling the story about when you were bullied in eighth grade and how you felt about it will go a long way toward getting your teen to open up about their own problems.

Lastly, create more opportunities for them to talk by following their interests a bit more. (See *Dad's Great Advice for Parents of Teens #11*, "Find New Ways to Connect with Them," in this book.) The more involved you are in their life and activities, the more opportunities you'll have to develop a meaningful conversation.

Once you've successfully achieved the impossible feat of getting your teen to talk with you, be careful not to ruin all your hard work by committing the number one sin a parent can make with a teen who is immersed in conversation. Never, under any circumstances, show any sign, hint, or whisper of the number one teen conversation killer…

Judgment.

Put yourself in your teen's shoes for a moment. They screwed up and did something stupid or embarrassing. They want to share it with you and get some help and advice, and maybe even some relief and comfort, but they feel so embarrassed and upset about it, they can barely bring themselves to tell you. But after you put on a wonderful display of all your amazing conversational ninja skills, they finally drop their defenses and blurt out the details of what they did. And then they reluctantly glance up at your face, and there's a moment that seems to move in slow motion and last a lifetime. How is their parent going to react?

And that's the moment of truth for you as a parent. You could do what comes naturally and explode in anger at their stupidity, but here's the big problem with that: Why would they ever bring their problems to you again when the first thing they expect to get from you isn't help and advice, but judgment? And if the first thing they feel after sharing their problem with you isn't relief and comfort, but shame and regret?

So instead of doing what comes naturally and alienating your teen in the process, do what comes unnaturally, avoid the number one parenting sin, and save your judgment of your teen for a later time.

You should notice that I said "save" your judgment of your teen; and using the word "save" was intentional. There are certainly times when it's appropriate to judge your teen, to point out to them when they've done the wrong thing or taken the wrong path, and make sure they know that they need to do better in the future. However, you need to be especially sensitive about when you do that, and especially clever about how you do that. While I can't tell you exactly when the right time to offer your judgment of them is, I can tell you that it's definitely not in the moments immediately after they shared their mistake with you. Those are the moments when you should save your judgment for later and instead offer them empathy.

"But somebody needs to tell them that they screwed up so they can learn from their mistakes!" you say.

Well, even though their poor little teen brains aren't fully developed yet, they know when they've made a mistake. They may do stupid things, but that doesn't make them stupid. Don't feel the need to point out to them what they already know. Don't feel the need to immediately judge them.

Of course, in one of life's cruelest twists, it turns out that the number one sin a parent can make with a teen also happens to be the number one hardest challenge for a parent to avoid. Thankfully though, there are many tips you can follow to make it easier.

First, before you react at all, take a moment or two and just absorb whatever it is your teen just told you. The longer you can delay your immediate gut reaction and remain silent, the better chance you have of responding in a more rational, productive manner.

Second, remind yourself of all the ways you definitely should NOT react. When your teen drops the bomb on you that they did something stupid, don't say things like, "How could you do that?!" or "What were you thinking?!" or "You really screwed up!" Even more importantly, don't give them that look that they teach parents in Parenting 101 classes, the one where you roll your eyes, shake your head, look disappointed, and let out a loud, exasperated sigh. That's the equivalent of saying, "What were you thinking?!" which is off limits.

What to do instead of judging and chastising them? Well... not much. But doing "not much" isn't that easy for parents. Doing "not much" means: Listen. Be sympathetic. Support them. Help them. Relax them. Calm them. Console them.

Instead of focusing on how disappointed in them you are, focus on how disappointed in themselves they must be, and have some empathy for how bad they must already feel. All you have to do is bite your tongue, listen, and find some way of being supportive.

Let them lead the conversation. Most importantly, recognize that by talking to you, most likely they just want their feelings validated, so do just that. Use phrases like "I'm so sorry to hear that," "That must not have been easy," "That must really suck," or even just "Really?!" or "I get it." Even if your teen is in the wrong in the situation they're describing, find something to pat them on the back for, and discuss the details at a later time. Find a way to be supportive in the moment.

Once they've started talking, pay attention to whether they're just looking for a sympathetic ear, or whether they want help with a problem. The cost of making a mistake and assuming the latter when they really want the former is extremely high, so if you can't tell, come right out and ask them: "Hey, do you want help with this, or do you just need somebody to listen?"

If they do tell you that they want help, don't just play the wise, experienced elder who knows everything and blurt out your advice as a fact. (Even though you and I both know that parents are indeed the wise, experienced elders who know everything!) Try to think the problem out with them by asking them questions and help lead them down the path to figuring out the solution themselves. (See *Dad's Great Advice for Parents of Teens #2*, "Teach Them How to Make Good Decisions," in this book.)

Assuming you master the art of saving your judgment of your teen, when is the right time to stop saving your judgment and start offering it? Well, you gotta know your audience. The right time to offer your judgment depends on when the sting of the mistake they made has dulled sufficiently, which is to say that it's probably sometime in the hours, days, weeks, months, or years after your teen shares their problem with you. And once you figure out the right time, the right way to offer your judgment is diplomatically and constructively. Perhaps even lean less toward offering judgment, and more toward trying to help them identify where they went wrong and how to do better in the future.

Is all this easy to pull off for a parent who just wants to help their teen out? Uh… no. Not easy at all. But certainly doable.

And if by some parenting miracle, you're able to pull it off, even just once, you're likely to see some quick results. For instance, just imagine your teen did something mildly careless, like getting a speeding ticket. Imagine the fear they must feel knowing that they have to tell you, with the expectation that you'll explode into some diatribe about how dangerous and unsafe it is to drive so fast. Your teen knows they can't avoid telling you, but they dread doing it. And now, imagine their surprise when, instead, you respond with a sympathetic smile and simply say, "That sucks. It must've been scary getting pulled over by the police. Are you doing OK?" Imagine the relief they must instantaneously feel when, instead of getting chastised, they get help.

It's a sense of relief that they'll remember for quite some time. They'll remember it long enough that, the next time they have an issue, they'll be much more likely to share it with you, because they know that instead of receiving judgment they'll receive empathy.

In the end, if you're thinking that it seems like a lot of work and strategizing to get these reluctant teens to open up to us, you're right. You might even start to wonder, "If they don't want to talk to me, why should I make them? They'll come talk to me when they're ready." Well, I would argue that all teens secretly want to talk more with their parents, especially about important matters that are bothering them, but their need for independence, and their need to prove themselves to their parents and to themselves, makes it particularly difficult to swallow their pride and open up. It's our job to open the lines of communication as much as we can and make it as easy as possible for them to come to us and share their lives when they're ready to. So the harder your teen shuts down, the harder you have to work to get them to talk.

Even if your teen has no interest in talking to their parents, you owe it to them to strategize in every way possible to make it as easy to talk to you as you can.

"Parenting teens is so often about having the good judgment to withhold one's better judgment."

–Robert Brault

FIND NEW WAYS TO CONNECT WITH THEM

Focus on the interests and activities your teen enjoys the most, and figure out how to participate in those interests to spend some quality time with them.

Remember the good old days when you'd have to run out to the grocery store, and you'd bring your child with you, and they'd have a great time just because they got to spend time with you? These days though, the probability of your teen accompanying you on a trip to the grocery store just to spend some quality time together is about equal to the probability of you getting struck by lightning... on a sunny day... while sitting in your basement... locked in a closet.

Your teenager no longer has any interest in participating in any of your interests and hobbies, and especially not your chores and responsibilities. After all, they have their own interests and hobbies, so why should they waste their time on yours?

At the same time though, it's important to remain connected to your teenager, especially as they get old enough to start having some adult interests—and adult problems to go with them. There are always the obvious mainstays to connect with a teen, like making sure you have dinner together as a family, or helping your teen with their homework (assuming you CAN help them with their homework—physics is hard!), but your teen is no rookie when it comes to avoiding their parents. They're experts at it!

So then how can you remain connected with your teen and involved in their life if you can't convince them to do anything with you? Well, as the saying goes, "If you can't beat them, join them." (And in this case, trust me, you can't beat them.)

"Joining them," though, involves learning to share your child's interests, and learning to love and enjoy those interests. (Or at the very least, learning to tolerate those interests.) That might mean binge watching all seventeen seasons of *Grey's Anatomy* together, or finishing the entire *Call of Duty* game on Xbox together, or even just drawing, reading, bowling, getting manicures, riding bikes, shopping, thrifting, or hiking together.

There are lots of options to choose from, but it pays to be strategic about which of your child's interests you get more deeply involved with. If they're into soccer, learn who Lionel Messi and Alex Morgan are and practice the game a bit. If they're into pop music, listen to some songs by Lizzo and Drake and learn the lyrics. If they're into TikTok, watch some videos by Charli D'Amelio and Zach King and learn some dances. For extra credit, secretly subscribe to or follow some teen-focused blogs, websites, newsletters, YouTubers, TikTokkers, Facebook pages, or subreddits to stay in the loop on who and what is popular with your teens. (Just don't let your teen find out!)

If your teen is the type who would get a kick out of helping you learn to get better at one of their interests, then you've got a lot more leeway in which activities you try to join them in. If they're not that type, then sharing the wrong interest with them might just become frustrating for them and do more harm than good. For instance, challenging them to a game of chess if you don't know a pawn from a rook probably won't be enjoyable for them. Joining them on a bike ride might not be fun for them if your top speed can only be described as "slower than grandma."

To protect against diving into the wrong interest with them in the wrong manner, either do some homework ahead of time to get up to speed and learn about their interest on your own, or pick something that doesn't require some skill or knowledge you don't have. For instance, it's easy to binge watch old episodes of their favorite TV show to catch up to the episode they're on, or secretly practice their favorite Xbox game at night to develop an understanding of the game. And it doesn't take a lot of expertise to hike, shop, read, or play a board game together with your teen.

The more familiar and comfortable you are with their activity, the more likely they are to share that activity with you. Remember though, that just because you spend a lot of time learning an activity, it doesn't mean your teen will immediately embrace doing that activity together. It might take some time for them to come around, and it might even require that you choose to do a different activity for them to come around. So be patient, and know that, with a little luck, your teen might actually learn to enjoy having you around to share their favorite activities with. And the more time you spend with your teen on their terms, the more time you have to connect with them.

Don't give up on trying to build a connection with your teenager. Focus on the interests and activities your teen enjoys the most, and figure out how to participate in those interests to spend some quality time with them.

"Stop trying to perfect your child, but keep trying to perfect your relationship with them."

–Dr. Henker

PROMISE THEM REAL UNCONDITIONAL LOVE

If your teen knows that nothing they do will ever cause you to love them any less, they'll feel a lot more comfortable being themselves, or asking for help when they need it.

"I love my child unconditionally."

If you're a parent, you've hopefully uttered this phrase a time or two, and hopefully within earshot of your kid. But have you given thought to what that implies? What it truly means at its core?

It's easy to love your child when they're being your perfect little angel. But what about when they're upsetting you? Or annoying you? Or outright pissing you off? What about when they fail, or mess up, or do something that you disapprove of? What about when they do something that brings shame to your family? What about when they betray you, or steal from you, or physically hurt you? Can you still love them even then?

Before you answer, let's be clear that if we're really taking the phrase literally, "unconditional love" means that you love somebody without conditions. You love them no matter what they say or do. But unconditional love doesn't mean unconditional approval. You can reject somebody's actions without rejecting them. And so...

Are you able to disapprove of your child's actions, but still love your child?

I believe the answer to that question for every parent should be... Yes. Every child deserves unconditional love from their parents. And every parent should be able to love their child even while they disapprove of the actions their child has taken.

Because the alternative to unconditional love is... conditional love. A love for your child that is conditioned upon them earning your love by doing a certain thing, or being a certain person, or saying a certain thing, or acting a certain way, or accomplishing a certain thing. If your child has to go through life with the constant pressure of knowing they need to earn your love by acting in a certain way, they're never able to feel the freedom to be the person they truly want to be. And that's a pretty crappy way to have to live your life.

Every human being deserves the security of knowing that, even if everything else in their life goes wrong, there will always be at least two people who love them, regardless of whether those people approve of the actions their child takes, or the choices their child makes, or the person their child becomes.

If you agree, make that promise to your teen. Promise to love them unconditionally. To love them truly without conditions. No matter what. No exceptions.

Make sure they know that they don't have to (and can't) earn your love by doing something, saying something, being someone, or acting a certain way. Make sure they know that you will always love them, not because of what they do, or who they've become, but simply because they're your child.

Unconditional love means you love them even when they piss you off, even when they get bad grades, even when they dent your car, even when they get suspended from school, even when they say they hate you, and even when they vape. Unconditional love means you love them even when they get arrested, even when they pursue a career you disapprove of, even when they steal from you, even when they lie to you, even when they love somebody you disapprove of, even when they embarrass you, and even when they let you down over and over.

Unconditional love does not mean that you give your teen anything they want and set no boundaries for them. Unconditional love does not mean you don't discipline them and punish them. Unconditional love does not mean that you never get irritated by them, or feel like you want to kick them out of the house, or actually kick them out of the house if that's what's best.

It's perfectly natural and human to be annoyed with or irritated by your teen from time to time, or even most of the time. And you might even find that there are times when you don't want to be around them, or when you don't even really like them all that much. If you happen to have those feelings, you're in good company with lots of other parents. The key thing to remember is that, regardless of what anger or annoyance or irritability you feel with your teen, you make it clear that they are still loved.

Unconditional love for someone means that even when you don't like them, you still love them.

No. Matter. What.

"But how can I make it clear that I still love them when I can barely stand to be in the same room with them?"

It's actually not hard at all. One of the simpler ways of making sure your teen knows you love them is to always finish each day with a reminder of your unconditional love. For instance, let's say you get in a huge fight with your teenager, and unkind words are spoken by them (something about comparing you to a guy named Satan). Tensions are high. You and your teen have each taken a few hours to calm down, but you're still getting the silent treatment. And yet, on your way up to bed, you kiss them on the forehead (or at least try to before they violently pull away from you) and tell them, "I love you." You probably get absolutely no reaction.

And yet, they get the message. They know. They know that, even though you're angry with them, and they're angry with you, they are still unconditionally loved, and always will be.

Have a hard and fast rule that, no matter what happens during the day, right before you turn in for the night, you kiss your teen and tell them, "I love you." Even if you have to grit your teeth while you say it. No exceptions.

Is it sometimes hard to remember that you love your teen when you're in the middle of an enormous disagreement? Sure. But the stakes are pretty high.

My good friend Archimedes Clutterbuck loved his daughter, Cleopatra Clutterbuck, unconditionally and told her so many times. But when she turned fifteen and wanted to tell her father that she was gay and was dating another girl, she was worried. She knew Archie had some pretty strong cultural and religious beliefs against homosexuality, and she was worried that he would never speak to her again. In fact, she was so worried that she considered just trying to act heterosexual for the rest of her life despite what she felt deep down inside, at the core of her being. That would've been a disaster, a truly awful way to live.

When Cleo finally worked up the nerve to tell him, Archimedes wasn't happy about it, and wasn't really able to hide it from her. He admitted to her, "It's not the life I want for you, and it's not a lifestyle that I approve of." And yet, moments later, when the tears were done flowing, Archie kissed his daughter on the cheek and told her, "I still love you, and I always want you to be happy."

It probably wasn't the best reaction possible, but he certainly did make sure Cleo knew that, even though he didn't support her lifestyle, he still loved her unconditionally.

(And fortunately, although it didn't happen overnight, Archie eventually did come around to fully embracing both his daughter's lifestyle and her partner, and is now quite a vocal advocate for LGBTQ+ issues!)

Archimedes' story is pertinent not just for parents of LGBTQ+ children, but all parents, because there's not one parent out there whose expectations and hopes and dreams for their child ever matched up perfectly with reality. It's just that some expectations end up farther from reality than others. Regardless, it all comes down to this:

Even when they do something you disagree with or don't approve of, love your child.

If you want your teen to be secure with themselves and feel comfortable pursuing the things that are really at their core, you'll learn to love your teen unconditionally, and make sure they know that they truly are loved unconditionally.

A teen who truly knows that they have the unconditional love and acceptance of their parent, no matter who they become or what they do, is much more likely to feel secure enough to become the person they were meant to become, whether it's a person who identifies as gay or queer, a person who converts to a different religion, a person who pursues an unexpected career, a person who is gender non-conforming, a person who marries somebody much different from themselves, or a person who simply acts in a way that is counter to their parent's wishes.

Similarly, a teen who knows that they have the unconditional love and acceptance of their parent, no matter what mistakes they make or trouble they get into, is much more likely to feel secure enough to come to you for help when they need it, whether it's a teen who gambles too much, a teen who becomes addicted to drugs, a teen who steals, or even a teen who commits a crime that lands them in prison.

Knowing they will always have unconditional love from their parent is one particularly important foundational thing that every teen needs to help them make it through the teen years and beyond.

Give absolute acceptance of whoever your child turns out to

be, or wants to be, even if it's somebody you wouldn't normally accept. If your teen knows that nothing they do will ever cause you to love them any less, they'll feel a lot more comfortable being themselves, or asking for help when they need it.

"These six words can save your child so much unnecessary pain: 'I love you as you are.'"

–Scott Barry Kaufman

Share Your Problems with Them

Share some of your minor problems with your teen and they'll be more likely to share their own problems with you.

Teens have problems—lots and lots of problems. Sometimes those problems are serious ones, dealing with alcohol, or drugs, or depression, or anxiety. Other times, those problems fall into the category of "OMG, what if I'm too early to the party, and I'm the first person there, and I'm stuck making small talk with Alex, or worse, I have to sit all by myself with nobody to talk to and everybody thinks I have no friends, and then my friends find out and they don't want to hang out with somebody who looks like they have no friends, and then I actually really won't have any friends and I'll live a long, lonely life and die alone with my twelve cats."

Regardless of the severity of your teen's problems, one thing is for sure: Teens don't like sharing their problems with anybody, but *especially* not with their parents. In fact, if you were to rank the people that your teen is most likely to share their problems with, that list would look something like this:

People Your Teen is Most Likely to Share Their Problems With

1. Their best friend
2. Their other friends
3. A teacher or counselor
4. Some blogger they follow
5. The bagger at your local grocery store
6. Any random adult walking down the street
7. Their parents

It's understandable why teens aren't eager to share their problems with their parents: They don't want to let you down, and they feel like they want to be perfect in your eyes.

Believe it or not, even though you often disgust or embarrass your teen and they probably can't bear to look at you much of the time, they probably look up to you as a role model (Maybe. Sometimes.). And they probably hold you up on this pedestal because they have this unrealistic view of you as somebody who either doesn't have any problems of their own, or who has all the answers to their own problems and never gets stressed out.

They probably have this view because, if you're like most parents, you try to shelter your kids from the daily pressures of your life, and you don't share the stress over making the rent payment, or the arguments with your spouse, or not getting the promotion at work, or even your general anxiety about life. They probably aren't aware of most of the problems you face, or most of the stress you deal with.

In general, not sharing your major problems with your teens

isn't a bad policy. Your job is to protect them and give them emotional support, not burden them with your own adult problems.

However, shielding them from 100% of your daily pressures comes with a major drawback: your teens form an unrealistic perception of the life of an adult and might start to wonder, "How come my life can't be as easy and as problem-free as my parent's life?" And even worse, your teen then becomes less likely to share their own problems with you because you've modeled behavior that teaches them not to share their problems with other people, and that they should project the appearance of having no issues in their life.

Not a good end result.

It's good to share some of your problems with your teen, so that they can see firsthand that you're not perfect (even though they probably already remind you of that daily), that adults have problems too, and that you can tackle those problems head on and come out on the other side in one piece.

If they start to hear about your problems, they're much more likely to feel comfortable sharing their own problems with you without feeling like they're letting you down. The more they realize you're not perfect, the less they'll feel like they have to be perfect in your eyes, and the more likely they are to share their issues with you.

So share your problems with your teen. But...

Be very careful about which problems you choose to share.

In general, don't share with your teen any of your real, heavy-duty problems, especially ones that are still ongoing. Sharing those types of problems will make your teen wonder how those problems are going to affect their own life, which will cause even more stress for them. You don't want to put your child in the position of having to act like a parent, or even have the same worries as a parent. That's not healthy. You're only trying to model good problem-solving behavior for them, not trauma dump on them and burden them with more concerns than they already have. (Remember how worried they already are about arriving early to that party?)

Here are a few examples of some problems you probably should NOT share with your teen:

- We are going to get evicted from our house soon.
- I can't stand my spouse.
- I have a gambling problem.
- My boss is going to fire me.

So what problems SHOULD you share with your teen?

The best problems to share are problems that they can easily identify with, like problems you had when you were a teenager. You can also share current problems, as long as those problems won't affect your teen directly, and are not meaningfully significant. And while you're sharing your problems, make sure you share the solutions too, so your teen can see how you dealt with the issue and that most problems usually have acceptable solutions.

Here are a few examples of some problems that you probably SHOULD share with your teen:

Problems You Had As a Teen:

- When I was your age, I was bullied too. Here's how I handled it.
- When I was a teen, the person I was dating cheated on me, and I was devastated. But I put myself back out there and quickly met somebody new who I liked even more and who treated me with respect.
- I drank way too much when I was your age, and nobody was around to help me stop. I ended up

getting into a lot of trouble that took me a long time to recover from.

Problems You Currently Have:

- My boss gave me a lot of work this weekend. But here's how I'm going to juggle that work with our weekend plans.
- I bought a defective product from a store and they refuse to refund my money. Here's how I'm handling the issue.
- I'm stressed out about a presentation I have to give at work. Here's how I'm trying to deal with the stress.
- Somebody at work is being lazy and isn't pulling their weight as much as they could. Here's what I'm doing about it.

Those are all situations that give your teen an appreciation that adults have problems too (and had similar teenage problems when they were younger), without burdening them with unnecessary stress. Once your teen learns that it's OK not just to have problems, but to share those problems and talk about them with others, they'll become significantly more likely to actually do that.

Share some of your minor problems with your teen and they'll be more likely to share their own problems with you.

"*Do I want to be a hero to my son? No, I would like to be a very real human being. That's hard enough.*"

–Robert Downey Jr.

BE THEIR PERSONAL CHAUFFEUR

Chauffeuring your teen might be the best chance you have to get to know their friends and be more involved in what's going on in their life.

There are many important skills that an adult needs to develop once they become a parent: how to change a diaper, how to help with geometry homework when you don't remember anything about geometry, and how to remain patient in the face of overwhelming, practically inhuman, annoyances. But as you probably know by now, one of the most often-used skills that every parent learns to develop is how to act as the personal chauffeur to a child.

It might start with driving them to and from school, but it quickly escalates to driving to soccer games, music lessons, friends' houses, carnivals, movies, and thousands of other activities. It might not surprise you to learn that by the time a child reaches the age of sixteen, the average parent has driven them a total of 187,000 miles. Or at least, that's what it feels like to the average parent!

Thankfully, as kids move into their teenage years, their genetically pre-programmed instinct to start traveling in packs with other teens kicks in, just as it does in savage wolves, which probably isn't a coincidence. And since they're traveling in a pack, until the first member of that pack gets their driver's license, a parent usually gets stuck driving the pack around wherever they need to go, while the other lucky parents catch a break. The real question is which parent becomes the unfortunate sucker who gets locked into a minivan with seven teenagers passionately discussing which couple at school they "ship" the most. (Teenspeak hint: "ship" loosely means "rooting for" in a romantic context.)

Usually there is some major strategic wrangling by the parents to try to offload as much of the driving responsibilities as possible onto the less strategically savvy parents. Excuses of being stuck in a meeting, feeling under the weather, having to work late, or the car being in the shop are all effective strategies for making sure some other parent/sucker steps up for driving detail.

However, I would urge you to reconsider your perfectly natural inclination to avoid becoming a personal chauffeur to a bunch of talkative teenagers. There happens to be one, and perhaps only one, advantage to driving teenagers around, but it happens to be a significant advantage: gathering intel.

If you happen to be one of those parents with the rare teenager who voluntarily shares with you all the details of what's going on in their life, then congratulations. But if you're in the remaining 99.9% of parents whose teens won't even share what they had for lunch, let alone where they're going, who they're hanging out with, and what they're doing, then you recognize the importance of learning more about your teenager's life to help guide and assist them. Ideally though, in all but the most serious of circumstances, it's best to respect your teen's privacy and not resort to snooping around their things or hacking into their phones and computers. And that's where being the chauffeur comes in.

When you pack a bunch of teenagers into a car with a parent present, an interesting thing often happens: They all shut up. They don't know how much the parent knows, or what it's appropriate to say around the parent, so they play it safe and just remain silent. It's like each teen feels like a perp brought in for questioning by the police, and nobody wants to be the one who says something to rat out their other friends, so they each exercise their right to remain silent. But in every pack of teenagers in a car, there's always a weak link in the bunch, and eventually (sometimes within seconds) one of the teens will bow to social pressure and break the silence. And that's when the floodgates of information open.

If you ever wanted to learn anything about what's going on in your teen's life, this is the moment. Keep your mouth shut and your ears open. If you have the means to hire a stenographer to sit in the front and take notes, I highly recommend you do so. Otherwise, just listen and take in as much as you can. You'll miss about 50% of what's said simply because it's impossible to understand the teen slang they're using and because they all talk at the same time, but there's a lot of value in what you can learn just from the 50% that you do take in.

For extra points, keep a Bluetooth earbud in your ear and pretend to be listening to a podcast. In the unlikely event that one of the teens in the car addresses you directly, ignore them completely and pretend like you're so involved in listening to your own podcast that you're barely paying attention to what all the teens are talking about. They'll want to believe you're not listening, and when they do, they'll completely let their guard down and let it all hang out.

Before your kid gets their driver's license and gains almost complete transportational independence from you, invest the time to be their personal chauffeur. In an ideal world, you'll never actually overhear anything concerning while driving your teen and their friends around town, and it will simply be one more way for you to get to spend time with (and potentially connect with) your child. However, listening to your teen's friends chatting during a car ride might be the best chance you have to be more involved in your teen's life and discover any significant issues going on that they're not comfortable sharing with you.

And if nothing else, you can actually have a few minutes to listen to that podcast.

Be more eager to be the parent who drives the kids around. Chauffeuring your teen might be the best chance you have to get to know their friends and be more involved in what's going on in their life.

"Nothing you do for your children is ever wasted."

–Garrison Keillor

DON'T DISCOURAGE THEM
FROM DATING OR SEX

*Relax and let your teen decide when they're
ready to start dating and having sex, and when
they do, support them as best as you can.*

A fellow dad once asked my good friend Archimedes Clutterbuck if his teenage daughter was dating anybody. Archie pulled the stereotypical father move and replied, "No, I'm keeping the boys away from her until she's thirty-two years old." Obviously, it was a joke, but the other father didn't think it was funny.

We all know the stereotypical "overprotective father" story (which applies to many moms as well):

The doorbell rings. Dad opens the door to a gangly, awkward teenage boy, who smiles up at him and asks if his daughter is home. Dad invites the young boy in, directs him to sit on the couch, and sits down in a chair in front of the fireplace, ensuring that the nervous teen notices the wall above the fireplace, upon which Dad's 10-gauge shotgun and the stuffed head of a grizzly bear are mounted. Dad gives the boy the third degree, asking about his background, if he has a job, if he's dated other girls, what his address is, and what the boy's intentions are with his daughter. As the boy stutters, Dad lets him know that if anything were to ever happen to his daughter, he knows where the boy lives, and then pointedly glances up to admire his shotgun. The young boy runs out the door crying, and when Dad's daughter walks into the living room asking where the young boy went, Dad merely gives an innocent shrug.

This tired old "overprotective father" story used to be symbolic of a loving parent, willing to do whatever was required to protect their child. However, we now know it to be a terribly sexist, damaging story, the message of which is unmistakable: "I don't think my teenager is ready to date yet. I don't think she is able to make her own decisions about her body. And I think she needs protection, not just from sexual assault, but from the possibility of engaging in safe, consensual sex that threatens to ruin her 'purity.'"

This message isn't damaging just to girls, but to every teen. Lots of parents of teenagers (regardless of their gender) are interested in delaying or pushing off their teen's dating life (and especially their sex life) for as long as possible.

But why? If your teen is interested in dating, and they feel that they're ready to become romantic with others, and maybe even have sex, why would you assume they're not ready?

After all, how are you really supposed to accurately judge whether your teen is ready to date or have sex? Unfortunately, there are no internationally agreed upon signs that will tip you off, and there isn't really any scientific way to determine when somebody is "ready" to date or have sex. (Technically there is a scientific way, and it's called puberty—but most parents I know wouldn't want to accept that milestone as the signal that their kid is ready to date or have sex!)

You can always depend on the good ol' reliable "I just know my kid and, trust me, they're not ready," argument, but as arguments go, it's not a very convincing one. In fact, the only reliable signal that indicates when your teen is ready to date or have sex is… when they tell you they are ready.

When it comes right down to it though, you gotta ask yourself:

Do you really think your kid isn't ready to date or have sex? Or is it possible (or likely, even) that they are ready, but the person who REALLY isn't ready is… you?

Try to put yourself in their shoes. Think back to how young you were when you started dating and having sex. Recognize that, no matter how old or young you were, the fact of the matter is that a lot of teenagers across the world are dating and having sex. The average age that most people lose their virginity in America is now about seventeen. And before you make some sexist assumptions, let me clarify that the average age that males lose their virginity is about seventeen, while the average age that females lose their virginity is… also about seventeen. (Worldwide, the average by country ranges from about seventeen to about twenty-three.) If you ignore when teens are actually having sex and instead focus on the age that teens are having sexual urges, the average drops to fifteen years old. So regardless of what your own values and norms are, realize that, if your teen is showing interest in dating and sex, they're in good company.

Before trying to impose restrictions on your teen, ask yourself a few questions: How old were you when you started to "like" someone romantically? How old were you when you started to date or "hang out" with others? How old were you when you had sex for the first time?

And more importantly, when you did start having sex, did you feel "ready"? Did you enjoy it? Do you think you started too early? Were your early sexual experiences positive ones? Do you have positive memories of it? Was it fun for you?

If you did start dating or having sex when you were a teenager, and it was indeed a positive experience for you, why would you expect that it would be any different for your teenager? Or more to the point—if your teen thinks they're ready, wouldn't you want them to enjoy their romantic and sexual experiences as much as you did?

On the other hand, maybe your answers to the above questions weren't quite as positive. Maybe you didn't date and become sexually active until later in life. Maybe your first experiences with dating or sex were miserable or traumatic. Even then, it doesn't make sense to let your own experiences color your attitude toward what's right for your teen. Just because you waited until later in life to date or have sex doesn't necessarily mean that's the right thing for your teen. Similarly, just because you had negative experiences with dating or sex doesn't mean that your teen will too.

In fact, when it comes to dating and sex, I can almost guarantee that your teen has absolutely no interest in knowing what worked or didn't work for you when you were younger. They only care about what's right for them. And that's what should drive you too: what's right for them.

Despite the fact that you and your teen may share half of your genetic data, your teen happens to be a completely different person than you. They're maturing at a different rate than you did, and have different feelings on a different timeline than you did.

More to the point, when it comes to dating and sex, your teen is going to find a way to do whatever they want, primarily because, when you're dealing with dating and sex, you're dealing with one of the strongest biological urges there is (multiplied by a thousand for a teen!), and not even a strict parent can compete with that.

In the end, when your teen tells you they're ready to date or have sex, you have three options available to you.

1. **Don't allow it, and fight it every step of the way.**
    A lot of parents go with this option. And it usually results in lots and lots of loud, screaming arguments, and a teen who finds a way to date or have sex anyway. You should know that abstinence-only programs and policies have been proven to be completely useless when it comes to

delaying when a teen becomes sexually active. Not only that, they've also been shown to stigmatize sex, reinforce harmful gender stereotypes, and worst of all, cause teens to be unprepared when it comes to avoiding unwanted pregnancies and sexually transmitted infections. In general, fighting the natural course of nature is a terribly ineffective strategy.

2. **Allow it and provide support and guidance.**
   If you don't try to stand in the way of your teen wanting to date or have sex, you retain the opportunity to encourage them to do so responsibly and take things slowly. Your teen will be more likely to share with you if they ever feel uncomfortable or pressured about the way things are progressing in their relationships, and you'll be in a better position to discreetly make sure your teen has access to condoms and contraception. Plus, acknowledging that your teen has some control over their life, while they're still able to feel comfortable moving at their own pace, might actually be just the difference between making dating or sex a positive or negative experience for them.

3. **Live in ignorance.**
   Ignorance is bliss. And for a lot of parents, living in ignorance is actually the best option. If you're the type of parent who wants to get on board and be supportive of your teen, but you just can't quite bring yourself to even think about them dating or, god forbid, having sex, then just ignore the whole situation. Just pretend that your teen isn't dating anybody. Don't ask them for details you can't stand to hear, don't ask them what's going on with their social life, and try to ignore any signs of a relationship you see. Sure, it's

not the healthiest reaction in the world, but if it's all you can muster, it's probably the best alternative for both you and your teen.

"So your Great Advice is to encourage my teen to start dating and having sex?!"

Nope. That would be silly. And more than a bit weird. Please don't actively encourage your teen to date or have sex. Instead, if your teen feels, all on their own, that they're ready to date or have sex, support them and help them think it through and make the right decision for themselves. Don't try to change their mind or convince them to live by your values and your timeline.

And especially don't try to dissuade them by trying to turn dating and sex into some scary, taboo, negative thing for them. First, that's just asking for future therapy bills. Second, it really isn't, and shouldn't be, something scary, taboo, or negative. If anything, it should be the opposite. Your teen's love life could be one area of their life that brings them the most happiness over the years. It should be something exciting and positive that brings them joy and happiness, not shame and fear—and especially not shame and fear from their parent.

Embrace your teen's interest in dating, and try to teach them how to date smart, by choosing the right partners for themselves with the qualities they care about. (See *Dad's Great Advice for Parents of Teens #19*, "Help Them Figure Out Who to Date," in this book.) And of course, if they choose to have sex, make sure they're practicing safe sex by using a condom every time, all the time. (See *Dad's Great Advice for Teens #23*, "Remain a Condom Virgin", in the *Dad's Great Advice for Teens* book.)

Lastly, even though our society has some pretty darn sexist beliefs when it comes to how many sexual partners somebody should have over their lifetime, don't make matters worse by perpetuating those beliefs. While not many parents are encouraging their teen to have multiple sexual partners, you want to be careful not to frame having multiple sexual partners as something that's shameful either. That's not typically a huge issue for most boys, but our sexist society puts so much pressure in that area on girls that there's now a name for it: slut-shaming.

Regardless of your own sexual experiences, the fact is that there are many people in this world who have had sex with somebody they weren't in love with, or somebody they didn't plan to marry, or maybe even somebody they met that night and never saw again, and didn't regret the experience. Is it the smartest thing in the world to have a one-night stand? Probably not. But is it something that ruins your life if you don't catch anything from it or cause any unwanted pregnancies? Probably not. So keep your judgment to yourself and make sure you don't slut-shame your own child.

Relax and let your teen decide when they're ready to start dating and having sex, and when they do, support them as best as you can.

"*A lot of parents will do anything for their kids, except let them be themselves.*"

–Banksy

TEACH THEM LIFE SKILLS

Prepare your teen for the real world by making sure they know the most important life skills they'll need once they're independent.

Remember how utterly helpless your child was when they were first born? They couldn't do a single thing for themselves except poop and throw up every once in a while. You had to teach them how to talk and walk (and now they often use that information to talk back to you and walk away from you). Their teachers at school taught them the very important skills of reading, writing, and multivariable calculus (I'm still hoping that comes in handy one day).

Despite what our teenagers may believe in their hearts, there's still a lot that they don't know. They're still helpless when it comes to some of the everyday life skills that most people need to survive. If you send them off into the world without teaching them some of these skills, you're doing them a disservice. So make sure you teach your teenager the most important life skills they need to become independent.

There are a couple of problems with this, though. The first problem is that you might not have learned some of these life skills yourself! The good news is that all you have to do is stay one step ahead of your teenager and learn the skill before trying to teach it to them. Learn a skill on Saturday, and teach it to your teen on Sunday. And in case you're wondering, you're a parent, so feel free to omit any mention of the fact that you learned the skill mere hours earlier and simply act like you're an expert who has years of experience with the skill. That's the parenting way!

The second problem is that there are so many life skills that a teenager needs to learn to become independent that you could fill an entire book with all of them (and in fact I have: *Dad's Great Advice About Life Skills for Teens*). But no need to read an entire book! Just focus on the most important teen skills, which I've boiled down for you here, into a list of the top twenty things you should make sure you teach your teenager.

Teach your child how to:

1. **Do Laundry**
    If you've spoiled your child by doing the laundry for them their entire lives, it's time that ends. And if they're too lazy to separate the whites from the colored clothing, just tell them to wash it all in cold water and they'll probably be fine.

2. **Use a Fire Extinguisher**
    The worst time to learn how to use a fire extinguisher is when there's a fire. Buy a cheap fire extinguisher, take your teen somewhere remote, and let them pull the pin and actually spray the extinguisher. It'll probably be the only time in their life when they actually get to use a fire extinguisher. Hopefully.

3. **Defend Themselves**
    Teach your teen that the two most valuable self-defense skills are how to talk your way out of a conflict, and how

to run away from one. But if those two aren't options, teach them the basic skills of how they can defend themselves. They should know that the most vulnerable spots on a person are the throat, nose, and, for males, the crotch. For extra credit, enroll them in a self-defense course tailored to teens.

4. Change a Car Tire

These days, it's true that fewer and fewer of our kids will be getting their driver's licenses. Even still, knowing how to change a tire is still important enough and easy enough that it's worth making sure your kid knows how to do it.

5. Jumpstart a Car

Easier than changing a tire, and even more useful, especially once they have kids of their own who constantly leave the interior car lights on and drain the battery.

6. Swim

If your teen is one of the estimated 20% of kids who don't know how to swim, it's time you changed that. It's a pretty serious safety issue, and it's a skill that's easily learned with just a little bit of time. Buy your teen a killer swimsuit and enroll them in a swimming class.

7. Bike

Although it's not quite as big a safety issue as swimming, riding a bike is still something everybody should know how to do. Make sure your teen isn't the exception to this rule.

8. Shave

Whether your teen is ready yet to shave their face, legs, or any other hairy areas they want to turn smooth, someday they will be ready, and it would be nice if you gave them a few tips on how to do so with a minimum of cuts and razor burn. Although there are many schools of thought, the general consensus is to keep things wet and lubricated with shaving cream or soap, and to shave with the grain of the hair, not against it. And here's a tip that not many people heed: rinse the razor after each and every swipe.

9. Keep Up with Personal Grooming

No, it's not fun to discuss things like body odor, flossing, tooth brushing, showering, menstrual cycles, or jock itch... but it's better than leaving them clueless about how to keep those issues under control. Have the discussion, even if it's uncomfortable.

10. Find and Reset a Breaker Panel

It's good for teens to know how their residence is powered, so show them where the breaker panel (or if you're old school, the fuse box) is, what circuit breakers look like when they're tripped, and how to reset them. While you're at it, show them where the water heater is, and where the gas and water shutoff valves are for your home as well.

11. Manage Their Time

Kids that are disorganized and have trouble managing their time and priorities turn into adults with those same issues. Getting your teen set up with a simple task list and calendar app can go a long way toward helping kids stay on top of the ever-growing list of responsibilities and deadlines they have to deal with.

12. **Manage Their Money**

There's a lot to this one, but get a head start and at least begin with the basics. The best single habit to help them build? Save half of everything they earn, put it in a separate account for retirement, and live below their means. That's one of the building blocks of the F.I.R.E. movement, which stands for Financial Independence, Retire Early. It's a great strategy for a teen to start internalizing, because living below their means and having a significant amount of savings is the best way to make sure that they can always walk away from a job or a situation that is less than ideal. They'll thank you for it when they're older.

13. **Organize Their Digital Files**

The older they get, the more electronic garbage your teens are going to produce. And the typical teen's filing system can often be summed up by "Put it all in the documents folder." Help your teen come up with a system of folders and subfolders that will help them keep their digital life organized for years to come. And while you're at it, help them set up a file backup system so that their files are protected even if (or when) their laptop or phone unexpectedly dies.

14. **Cook**

It's pretty clear by now that frozen, processed foods aren't nearly as healthy as freshly cooked meals. At the very least, make sure your kids know how to cook simple, healthy meals in a way that makes them eager to eat those meals, rather than dread them.

15. **Be an Autodidact**

If you don't know what an autodidact is, take a moment to look up the term right now. I'll wait... Great! I've just turned you into an autodidact. Now, do everything in your power to teach your teen how to be an autodidact as well (ironic, I know). Make sure they know that they are amazingly lucky to be among the first generation in the history of the world who can, in just seconds, find instructions and step-by-step videos on how to do just about anything a human being could imagine wanting to learn how to do.

16. **Take Care of Basic First-Aid**

There are some non-emergency health issues that you should prepare your teen to deal with. Teach them how to treat a basic cut (with antibacterial cream and bandages) and a minor burn (with cortisone or aloe). Make sure they know when and how to perform CPR, and how to help a choking victim with the Heimlich maneuver. More importantly, teach them how to judge whether something is worthy of a visit to the doctor, urgent care center, or emergency room, or if it requires a 9-1-1 call.

17. **Be Alone**

If there's one thing that is kryptonite for teens, it's being alone. Even standing alone for a few moments at a party can make a kid feel self-conscious. Which is a shame, because feeling confident enough to be alone for a few minutes, hours, or even days, is a powerful feeling. Make sure your teen learns to become comfortable being alone.

18. **Speak Like an Adult**

Uh... so, like, a lot of teens have trouble, um, putting a sentence together that is... you know... uh... so... yeah.

Teach your kids that, if they want to interact in the real world with adults, they have to put aside their "teenspeak" and speak with confidence as an adult.

19. Travel

Someday, your teen may be traveling on their own, and doing so can be a bit overwhelming. Next time you travel with your teen by plane, train, or bus, have them lead the way through the whole process. Let them figure out where to check in, how to check their bags, how to make it through security, what gate to go to, and when to board.

20. Use Tools

Teach your teen how to use a basic set of tools and what each tool is for, so they're able to fix simple things that pop up from time to time. Every teen should know how to use a power drill, adjustable wrench, Allen wrench, screwdriver, pliers, saw, and a hammer. Extra credit if you also teach them how to properly use a jigsaw, circular saw, and rotary tool.

Prepare your teen for the real world by making sure they know the most important life skills they'll need once they're independent.

"It is not what you do for your children, but what you have taught them to do for themselves, that will make them successful human beings."

–Esther Pauline Lederer ("Ann Landers")

HAVE A CODE WORD TO BECOME THEIR SCAPEGOAT

Agree to play the villain around your teen's friends, and help your teen avoid uncomfortable or dangerous situations.

Imagine your teen is at a park, late at night, with dozens of other teenagers. They're all having good, clean, fun, until one of the teens suggests they spray paint graffiti all over the park walls. Most of the teens think it's a fun idea, and one of them goes home to get the paint. Your teen's friends are all into it, and are asking your kid, "What are you going to write?" To your child's credit, they don't want any part of this. They think it's wrong and mean, not to mention illegal, and could land the whole group of them in jail.

But thinking that is easy. Acting upon it requires a lot more strength.

Your teen runs through their options: Speaking up and saying that the group shouldn't do it would just annoy everybody and wouldn't convince anyone. Just walking away would get your teen out of the situation, but then they'd be viewed differently, and ostracized for being afraid, or for not wanting to be part of the group. Staying and not participating still puts them at risk just for being at the scene of the crime, and still causes them to get teased and harassed for not joining in on the fun. Joining in and partaking in the graffiti feels wrong, but it's the safest, easiest, option, and they probably won't get caught if they're lucky.

The kid returns with the paint. It's decision time.

Somebody holds out a can of spray paint, offering it to your teenager. Your teen hesitates, but in the end, they make their decision. They decide to…

Suddenly, tires SCREECH to a halt as you pull up in your car, honk the horn, and loudly yell, "Aunt Eunice has taken a turn for the worse. You need to come home right now!" Your teen looks furious at you for ruining all the fun, and mutters to their friends, "I hate my parents! But you know how it is. I gotta go." Their friends all nod in agreement and pat your teen on the back, feeling sorry that they have to miss out because they have such overbearing parents.

Your kid hops in your car, and slams the door angrily, yelling, "Why can't you ever just let me have any fun?!" loud enough for the whole neighborhood to hear as you pull away. You both sit in silence for a few moments as you head home.

Moments later, at a stoplight, your teen turns to you, smiles, and says, "Thanks."

At some point in their life, your teen is probably going to get into a sticky situation where they know exactly what they should do, but might not have the guts to actually do it. They want to do the right thing, but don't want their friends to know. If only they had a scapegoat they could blame it on…

That's where you come in.

As their parent, you have the power and authority to demand that your teen does as you say and comes home the moment you demand it. Once you stop laughing hysterically at that thought, let me point out that even though you, me, and the rest of the parenting world knows how absurd that idea is, your kid's friends probably don't. And that means that you can serve as the perfect scapegoat for your child when they need help getting out of a sticky situation.

In order to play your role and act as that scapegoat, you need to be aware of when to jump in to play your part. But how? How did you know to drive up to the park at the exact moment you did? And how did Aunt Eunice's illness take a turn for the worse at just the right time?

Don't worry. Aunt Eunice is fine. It was all a ruse.

You were able to swoop in just in the nick of time because you set up a "code word" with your teen ahead of time. Clever, eh?

When your teen is with all their friends, they can't always secretly get away to call or text you to ask you to come up with an excuse to make them come home. So you need to determine some signal ahead of time that your child can easily text you or work into a conversation on the phone, something that won't seem out of place to their friends but will indicate to you that they need an excuse to come home.

Here are some ideas for code words that your child could use:

- Ask how Aunt Eunice is feeling.
- Work a somewhat unique word into the conversation, like "frigid" or "monkfish."
- Use uncharacteristically proper grammar, such as "May I please stay out a bit later tonight?"
- Say particularly mean things about their parent, like "I really hate you right now." (Though this one doesn't work so well if your child regularly says particularly mean things about you!)

Admittedly, teaching your child to make up a lie to get out of an uncomfortable situation isn't exactly what we teach in Parenting 101. It's not a great example to set. And ideally, we all want to raise children who have the strength and self-confidence to simply walk away from a bad situation, without any regard for what their friends might think. Or better yet, not become friends in the first place with hooligans who are going to drag them into negative situations. But if you live in the real world, you realize how hard it is to be a teenager today, and that it's not always easy for them to do the right thing.

So make it easier for them to do the right thing. Set up a code word with your teen that signals to you they want you to make them come home. Agree to play the villain around your teen's friends, and help your teen avoid uncomfortable or dangerous situations.

"A hero is someone who has given his or her life to something bigger than oneself."

–Joseph Campbell

DON'T TELL THEM WHO TO DATE

It's hard enough for a teenager to find the "right one" when it comes to dating, so don't make it harder by adding your wishes to the mix.

When he was a teenager, my good friend Archimedes Clutterbuck secretly dated a girl for several years. It was a secret because the girl came from a traditional Indian family who expected her to only date and marry traditional Indian boys, and, as you might be able to tell just from his name, Archimedes is neither Indian nor anything even close to traditional.

It was hard on the girl, not just because of the pressure her parents put on her, but because her brother stepped right into line and married a traditional Indian woman who fit the parents' profile perfectly. But Archie and his girlfriend were in love, so years later, they revealed their secret relationship to the family and, against the wishes of his wife's parents, got married. He was eventually welcomed into the family, but let's just say it wasn't exactly with open arms.

A decade later though, the parents changed their tune. The traditional Indian woman that the brother married revealed herself to be an awful person who stole jewelry from her mother-in-law, treated her husband terribly, and put herself above everybody else in the family, including her own children. Archie, on the other hand, spent that decade treating his in-laws with deference and respect, and treating their daughter like a queen in every way.

It took years, but in the end, the parents thanked their daughter for thinking for herself and choosing her husband by focusing on his character rather than his culture. The parents eventually realized that there are qualities to look for in a mate that are much more important than just a person's background and heritage.

If you think back to your own teenage years, you probably remember that it was pretty hard to figure out what type of person you wanted to date, let alone what it was you were looking for in a mate. It's hard enough for a teen to determine exactly which qualities are the ones that they care about when it comes to making a decision about who to date and who not to date. Don't put even more pressure on them by adding more criteria to their decision, particularly when those criteria involve the color of a person's skin, the country their ancestors came from, or the religion that their parents raised them under.

It's understandable why some parents put pressure on their children to date others within their own culture or religion. "It's just easier when two people share the same heritage," some parents claim. But as you can tell from my friend Archie's experience, this isn't always true. Instead, to be more specific, I would say it's easier when two people share the same *values*, which sometimes comes from sharing the same heritage, but not necessarily. It's just that many parents tie particular values to their own heritage: "Our religion values family more than others, which is important to us," or "Our culture emphasizes the importance of education and improving our world."

However, as my friend Archie's in-laws discovered the hard way, even if your culture does in fact represent some positive characteristics overall, not every person who belongs to that culture is going to fit the profile. There are a lot of people who serve as terrible exceptions to the rule in every culture and religion.

And let's just put all the cards on the table and be completely honest: Some parents want their kids to settle down with somebody from within their own race, culture, heritage, or religion simply because they think their particular group is just "better" than others. If you think this attitude is a bit racist or narrow-minded, I'd agree with you. However, you might be shocked to learn that science says there actually IS a particular race out there that is more likely to have some of the more positive attributes that society values. Which race is it?

Well, it's not one particular race, per se, but rather, multiple races. To be more specific, scientific studies have shown that, when compared to babies from couples with the same race or heritage, mixed-race or mixed-heritage babies are more likely to be taller, be more intelligent, be more conventionally attractive, and achieve a higher level of education.

So I guess your heritage might not be the "best" one after all. And if you want your grandkids to be tall, smart, beautiful, and go to graduate school, perhaps you should be encouraging your teen to date somebody from a different background.

In addition to all that, the whole argument that "it's just easier for couples when they share the same heritage" isn't necessarily true. When it comes right down to it, it's not very hard for a mixed-heritage couple to figure out how to celebrate both Christmas AND Ramadan, or how to visit distant relatives in both Denmark AND Vietnam. Those are problems easily solved just with some good planning, discussion, and scheduling.

On the other hand, it is significantly harder for a couple to find a middle ground when one person believes it's OK to lie and cheat to get ahead and the other believes honesty is the best policy, or when one believes that homeless people are lazy and should just get a job and the other believes we should help people less fortunate than ourselves. Those are real issues that can cause real problems for a couple.

It's hard enough for a teen to find a person they like who shares important positive qualities like good values or intelligence or humor, so don't make it even harder for your teen by trying to convince them to focus on more meaningless qualities like skin color, the god they worship, or the name of the country their ancestors came from. Otherwise, you risk pushing your teen into focusing so much on finding a partner who shares their heritage that they're willing to overlook the fact that perhaps they don't share more important personality traits that contribute a lot more to a healthy relationship. Or to put it more succinctly:

The more pressure you put on your teen to date somebody from their same heritage, the more likely they are to overlook the important stuff and end up dating a total jerk.

It might be hard for you to avoid putting pressure on your teen about who they should date, especially if your heritage is an integral part of your identity and who you are. If so, just practice saying the following phrase in the mirror: "I don't care who you date, as long as they treat you well and make you happy."

And then, any time the subject comes up with your teen, or when they ask you about some romantic interest in their life, simply say to them, "I don't care who you date, as long as they treat you well and make you happy."

And when you're alone, thinking about your teen and their dating life, and worrying about the person they're spending time with romantically, repeat to yourself, "I don't care who they date, as long as the person treats them well and makes them happy."

It's hard enough for a teenager to find the "right one" when it comes to dating, so don't make it harder by adding your wishes to the mix.

"*Cannot we let children be themselves, and enjoy life in their own way? You are trying to make another you. One's enough.*"

–Ralph Waldo Emerson

HELP THEM FIGURE OUT WHO TO DATE

Be smart about how you help your teen identify the qualities that matter to them when deciding who to date.

It's every parent's worst nightmare: Your teen is going on a date with somebody new, and when you get a chance to meet the person your teen is about to spend the evening with... well, they're awful. Really awful. They're the type of person you imagine kicks their dog when nobody's looking, or is rude to restaurant servers, or bullies other kids at school.

What are you supposed to do? Do you forbid them from going on their date? Do you tell your teen you think that person is a jerk? Do you shove the person out the door and send them on their way?

Sadly, the right answer here is... you smile and tell your teen to have a great time. And the reason you do that is because of Teen Parenting Secret Numero Uno, which almost all parenting experts agree upon:

If you don't approve of the person your teenager is dating, the last thing you should do is let your kid know that fact.

Why not? Well, have you ever heard of Romeo and Juliet? Nothing makes a potential dating partner more attractive to a teen than knowing that their parents disapprove of that person. It turns a boring, humdrum relationship into a secret, exciting, rebellious, dangerous, forbidden love. Unless you want to cement your teen's relationship even more with that person you disapprove of, keep it to yourself.

But don't worry! All is not lost! And there's still a big role for you to play in helping your teen make good choices about who to date, so you can avoid getting into a situation like this in the first place.

Although *Dad's Great Advice for Parents of Teens #18*, "Don't Tell Them Who to Date," dictates that you shouldn't push your teen toward dating somebody from a particular race, religion, background, or heritage, it certainly IS fine to try to guide your teen toward making their dating decisions by evaluating some of the more important qualities that contribute a lot more to building a healthy relationship.

It's entirely possible (perhaps even probable) that the qualities your teenager cares most about in the person they want to date are those qualities that one might diplomatically refer to as the more "superficial" qualities, such as beauty, wealth, or popularity. And when it comes down to it, there's absolutely nothing wrong with people who are beautiful, wealthy, or popular. It's just that there are other qualities that might be more important than beauty, wealth, or popularity. If your teen is trying to set themselves up to build a healthy romantic relationship, most people would agree that focusing on more intrinsic qualities is more likely to lead to success.

As a result, your job should be to try to steer them away from making their dating decisions based on things like the size of a person's muscles or breasts, and toward prioritizing things like the size of a person's heart or intellect.

But you can't just dictate a list of qualities to your kid that they should use in making their dating decisions. It's their dating life, not yours, and you should let them drive the process when determining the characteristics that they care about the most in a dating partner.

Guide your child toward determining the qualities they care about most by asking them pointed questions, like:

- "What personality characteristics are you looking for in somebody you date?"
- "What are some of the qualities that all your friends have in common? Are these qualities you care about in somebody you date?"
- "If you look at all the people you've been interested in dating, what do they all have in common?"

Your teen might want your help in the process, and just directly ask what qualities you think they should care about. Be careful. This could be a trap! If they know the qualities that you want them to care about, there's a chance that they'll end up looking for people who run counter to those qualities, especially if they're the rebellious type.

So rather than come right out and directly tell them what you think the most important qualities in a person are, ask them questions that lead the witness a bit more:

- "On a scale of one to ten, how do you rate the following qualities in terms of importance to you? Honesty, beauty, kindness, sense of humor, creativity, intelligence, popularity, adventurousness, optimism, wealth, altruism, curiosity, playfulness..."

If your teen ends up giving their highest ratings to some of the more "superficial" qualities mentioned earlier, don't panic. First of all, remind yourself that just because those are the qualities they care about as a teenager doesn't mean those are the qualities they're going to care about as an adult. In fact, there's something to be said for the common practice of people distinguishing between "the type of person you date" and "the type of person you marry." For many teens, they simply have to learn the hard way by dating a few jerks who only have superficial qualities before realizing that they should look for different, more important qualities in a partner.

With all that said, this might be the right opportunity to very subtly and diplomatically offer them your slightly different take on which are the important qualities to focus on. Consider sharing your thoughts in a general way that should sum it all up for them:

- "I think the single most important quality you should look for is whether or not they treat you with respect and kindness, and whether you feel like treating them the same."
- "I think the most important quality you should look for is whether they make you happy most of the time, and whether you make them happy most of the time."

While guiding your teen toward using the right criteria when choosing who they date is important, none of that does any good if they don't know how to accurately judge whether a person has those qualities. There are a lot of people out there that your teen might date who have mastered the art of sounding like they're sincere in expressing the things they care about, when what they really care about is something completely different (and usually that thing is… themselves). Said less diplomatically, there are some "fake" people out there who talk a good game.

Teach your teen the best antidote to use to identify those people: Focus on how a person acts, not what they say. (See *Dad's Great Advice for Teens #4*, "Don't Believe a Word Your Boyfriend/

Girlfriend Says," in the bonus section of this book.) It's easy for somebody to tell you they really care about you, but it's not nearly as easy to actually act in a way that reflects that.

Tell your teen to look for the telltale signs of somebody who really cares about them: They want to spend a lot of time with you and do things that make you happy.

And teach them to be on the lookout for some of the telltale signs of somebody who might not be as serious about the relationship: They only make plans with you at the last minute when they don't have anything else to do, and when they're with you, they often have to have things their way, rarely giving in or compromising.

The old proverb really is true: Actions speak louder than words. Remind your teen to not just look for the right qualities in the people they date, but evaluate whether the people they date really have those qualities by watching what they do, not just listening to what they say.

Let's face it though: Even if you guide your teen toward a very well-defined set of positive personality traits that they want to use when deciding who to date, and even if your teen becomes proficient at recognizing whether a person has those traits, the heart wants what the heart wants. And so there's still a possibility that your teen brings home that amazingly attractive person who kicks their dog when nobody is looking. What then?

Step one is to remind yourself of the aforementioned Teen Parenting Secret Numero Uno: If you don't approve of the person your teenager is dating, the last thing you should do is let your kid know that fact.

Step two requires a bit of finesse: You want to draw their attention to the qualities they've told you in the past that they care about, and ask them to weigh whether their dog-kicking date has those qualities. But you want to do so without weighing in with your own opinion in the matter. It goes something like this...

"I really like the person you're dating because they seem to make you happy, but I remember you saying that one of the qualities you look for in a partner is kindness. Well, when I saw them kick that dog the other day, I just thought I'd ask...do you think they're kind?"

Step three is simple: Let that question simmer. It might take days, or even weeks, but with any luck, drawing a bit of attention to the fact that their date doesn't really fit all the criteria they care about in a person might be all that is needed to get them to realize it.

And even if they don't realize it immediately, chances are they're going to realize it before any marriage vows are spoken. On the plus side, the longer they spend time with a person who doesn't have the qualities they want, the more they'll focus on those qualities when they're looking for the next person to date.

I should note, if your teen is in a relationship in which they're genuinely being mistreated or even abused, all bets are off. Some of the warning signs to look for that indicate the difference between somebody who is just a jerk and somebody who is psychologically abusive are: manipulative or controlling behavior, extreme jealousy or possessiveness, insults or disrespect, and online bullying or harassment. If your teen is in a relationship that shows any signs of mistreatment, forget all the subtlety mentioned above and jump in with both feet with a direct and forthright discussion with them. And if that isn't effective, enlist the help of a professional.

Don't tell your teen exactly what qualities they should look for in a person they want to date. That's something they need to do for themselves, although you can and certainly should help them figure it out. When you do, be smart about how you help your teen identify the qualities that matter to them when deciding who to date.

"I have found the best way to give advice to your children is to find out what they want and then advise them to do it."

–Harry S. Truman

TRUST THEM

Put more trust in your teen, and they're likely to rise to the challenge and become more trustworthy.

We all want to be able to trust our child. Trust them to be safe, trust them to make smart choices, and most importantly, trust them to be honest with us. And even though some kids hit the mark on trust more than others, it's probably safe to say that all teens really want to be trusted by their parents, simply out of respect.

It's important to realize that you, as a parent, play a not-so-insignificant role in your teen's trustworthiness. I might even go so far as to say that you are one of the most significant drivers of their trustworthiness. As much as we'd all like to say that the amount of trust we give our teens is driven by how they act, when it comes right down to it, in many cases it's exactly the opposite—how they act is driven by the amount of trust we give our teens. Trusting your teen can be a self-fulfilling prophecy. Parents who don't trust their teens create teens that can't be trusted.

Here's why: As teens get older, they're going to want more and more independence, and they're going to try to push the boundaries of that independence more and more. At some point, the boundaries that they're comfortable with are going to be different than the boundaries that you're comfortable with, and that's when the sparks start to fly—and when your reaction to that situation becomes important.

For example, let's say that your teen wants to go to a party, and there's going to be drinking at that party. You could respond one of two ways:

Response A

You tell them that because there is going to be drinking at the party, they're not allowed to go, because you don't want them drinking alcohol. So your teen stays home. The next day, they're bombarded with stories from their friends about how much fun the party was and what a great time they missed out on. The next weekend, your teen hears about another party, but knowing that there's no way you're going to let them go to this one if you didn't let them go to the last one, they lie, and tell you that they're going to their friend's house instead of the party. And once they've lied about the party, it's not a big leap to lie about drinking at the party, so they have a few drinks.

Response B

You tell them that because there is going to be drinking at the party, you don't want them to go because you don't want them drinking alcohol. But… you'll trust them to go to the party anyway if they promise not to drink while they're there. Your teen gets excited, not just because they get to go to the party, but also because their parent treated them as an adult and trusted them to make responsible decisions at the party. And sure enough, when they're at the party and somebody offers them alcohol, they remember the pride they felt when you put your trust in them, and they're much more likely to decide not to drink.

At some point in their teenage years (hopefully in the later years, rather than the earlier years) your teen is going to decide for themselves what they want to do, regardless of what you want. And when they do, either you're going put your trust in them that they're doing it responsibly, and hope that they tell you what they're up to, or you're going to try to stop them from doing it and create incentives for them to lie to you.

And if you think that you're such a clever, connected parent that you'll always find out about what your kids are up to, think again. Even if you're tied into the community, and know all your kid's friends' parents, and snoop through their stuff, you're still not going to know everything going on with your teen. And even if you did know everything going on with your teen, you still can't easily stop them from doing it anyway. Trust is kind of key.

The only surefire way to know what your child is up to is to trust them enough to tell you.

Create positive incentives for them to share the truth with you. One of the best ways of doing that is, when they do share the truth with you, don't punish them or overreact to what they shared with you (See *Dad's Great Advice for Parents of Teens #21*, "Let Them Make Stupid Mistakes," in this book.) If your teen trusts you enough to tell the truth about something difficult, reward them by not punishing them. Let the truth set them free, at least when it comes to punishment from you.

Another key to building trust with your teen is to make sure that, when you do put more trust in them, you clearly define the expectations of that trust. For instance, if you decide to trust them to stay out past their normal curfew, make sure they know that that doesn't mean they can stay out until six in the morning without checking in. Make it clear that if they're going to stay out for more than an hour past curfew, they need to call or text you with an update.

To be clear, trusting your child doesn't mean relieving them of the responsibility to share some of the details of their life with you. You're still their parent, they're still your child, they're still not adults, and there are still reasonable things you should demand from them.

There's a fine line between privacy, which your child is entitled to, and secrecy, which they're not entitled to.

For instance, it's not OK for your teen to keep secrets about where they are going, who they will be with, and when they will be back. However, they are certainly entitled to keep private exactly what they talked about at a party, or who they talked to.

And of course, remind your teen that, just as it is in the real world, the trust you put in them can be destroyed in an instant with just a small slipup on their part. If you catch your teen lying to you, it's appropriate to be less trusting of them in the future, and to punish them in some way—not for doing whatever it is they were hiding from you, but rather, for lying to you. Show your child what it's like not to have your trust, but make sure you eventually give them the opportunity to earn it back.

Put more trust in your teen, and they're likely to rise to the challenge and become more trustworthy.

"Strict parents raise the best liars."

–Unknown

LET THEM MAKE STUPID MISTAKES

Give your teen the opportunity to learn from their own mistakes, as long as the long-term consequences of those mistakes aren't too severe.

Scientists have shown that, diplomatically speaking, the rational part of a teenager's brain isn't fully developed until the age of twenty-five. In not-so-diplomatic terms, that means that teens can sometimes act stupid.

When they were younger and made stupid mistakes, you probably let them get away with the stupid mistakes that were small with less severe consequences, such as leaving the television on, or forgetting to put their dirty clothes in the hamper. But hopefully, you stopped them from making the really stupid mistakes with more severe consequences, such as sticking a fork into the power outlet, or leaning out over the balcony too far.

However, now that your child is a teenager, the consequences of stupid mistakes they make are little less predictable in nature. While even a teenager can accurately predict that sticking a fork into a power outlet is not going to feel very good, there are other mistakes they might make that will have consequences that aren't as easy for them to foresee, such as drinking too much, or speeding down the highway, or, god forbid, talking back to their parent.

And sometimes, even when they can foresee the possible consequences of a potential mistake, they predict the probability of those consequences happening to be zero, when in actuality, that probability is significantly higher than zero.

In short, teenagers think nothing bad will ever happen to them, and sometimes the only way to convince them that something bad might happen to them is… for that bad thing to actually happen to them. Some things they have to learn on their own, because they can't just take somebody's word for it, especially not the word of their parent. Or to put a more positive spin on it, they sometimes need to make their own mistakes simply to satisfy their own curiosity about the world.

So don't try to save your teen from every little stupid mistake that lies ahead of them. Part of trusting your teen is trusting them enough to let them make their own stupid mistakes. The big issue is which stupid mistakes to allow them to make, and which stupid mistakes are way too costly to allow them to make. Unfortunately, it's not so easy to determine.

One of the best ways to decide whether the stupid mistake your teen is about to make is too costly is by weighing the long-term effects of that stupid mistake (and being honest about the true long-term effects). I recommend you apply "The Hospital Test" when trying to evaluate which stupid mistakes to allow your teen to make: If the stupid mistake is likely to involve a hospital, the police, or going viral on the internet for the wrong reasons, then step in and put a stop to the stupidity. (See *Dad's Great Advice for Parents of Teens #2*, "Teach Them How to Make Good Decisions," in this book.)

You should be aware of the top two most common stupid mistakes teenagers make that fall into the category of having severe long-term consequences: auto-related stupid mistakes and drug-related stupid mistakes.

Half of all teenage deaths are attributable to unintentional injury, and most of those injuries (75%) are due to automobile accidents. After automobile accidents, the next most common cause of injury is drug use. So when it comes to cars and drugs, by all means, put a moratorium on the "Let your teen make stupid mistakes" outlook and insist that your teen is extra vigilant and errs on the side of caution. If your teen shows up high and asks for the keys to the car, the stupidity level is so extreme that you should step in and put a halt to the madness.

However… if the stupid mistake passes "The Hospital Test," consider letting the stupidity flow.

For example, letting your teen go out to a party on a Saturday night when they should be studying for the biology quiz they have on Monday morning could result in them flunking their quiz. And while that certainly won't help their biology grade, it also isn't going to be the single factor that leads to them not getting into college, not getting a job, and being homeless for the rest of their life. Instead of stepping in, perhaps you should point out the stupidity of trading their grade for their party, but let them make their own decision and live with the consequences. You never know—with some luck, maybe they'll ace the quiz anyway.

If you're fortunate, most of the stupid mistakes your teen makes will fall into the category of "That's a stupid mistake to make, but go ahead and make it because it will be a good learning experience for you and hopefully stop you from making that same stupid mistake again in the future."

Of course, someday the odds are likely to catch up with your teen, and it's possible they'll eventually make a stupid mistake that results in some real-world consequences that bite them hard in the ass. The big question is, what do you do in that case? What do you do when they get caught doing something so stupid that they're going to have a real price to pay to society in some way?

Well, here's what not to do: Don't punish them more. Don't yell at them. Don't say, "I told you so." Don't ask them, "What the hell were you thinking?" Don't tell them, "You're stupid for making that stupid mistake." And certainly don't abandon them or leave them to deal with their problem alone, even though they created the problem themselves.

"Don't punish them?!" I hear you cry, "How will they possibly learn if I don't punish them?!"

The purpose of a punishment is generally to create negative consequences and negative incentives for your teen so they don't ever make the same mistake again. If they make a stupid mistake but don't get caught in that mistake, a punishment from you may be entirely appropriate and constructive. However, we're imagining a scenario in which they do get caught making the stupid mistake and receive some sort of (hefty) punishment; that punishment just happens to not be coming from you.

All of us cynical adults already know how cruel this world can be, and how difficult life can get sometimes. But your teen is, hopefully, still in the dark about that. So when they make a stupid mistake, it might be the first time that they experience the world slapping them down, and that can be quite a painful shock to the system. Just realize that any punishment you could hand down to your teen after making a stupid mistake is probably going to pale in comparison to the punishment imposed by the world and to the real-life consequences of making that mistake.

They're probably feeling bad enough already about their stupid mistake. They're probably already dealing with what could be the worst possible punishment of all: shame. If so, you don't need to pile on. Nothing you do is going to make them feel worse than the "D" they get on the test because they stayed out too late at that party, or the court-mandated driving school they have to attend because of that speeding ticket, or the terrible hangover they have to nurse because of all that tequila they drank.

Rather than punishing your teen after the world has already

taken its pound of flesh, be there to support them. And if there's any childish sliver of your subconscious that feels even an ounce of "I told you so" glee, make damn sure you hide it. Instead, focus on showing how sad you are that they're getting a taste of how hard life can be. Show some empathy, and simply be there for your teen to help them get back on their feet. Promise them that you will help them get through this, and remind them that "It gets better," and that "This too shall pass," because both those sayings happen to be true—it does indeed get better, and the difficulties do indeed pass.

Essentially, you want to shift your role from being the enforcer, who is there to set rules and punish those who break them, to being the advisor, who is there to help console them and navigate them through the consequences of their mistakes.

Just be there for your teen. Nothing more.

After you've done that, then comes the risky part, which you should only attempt if you've already conquered the beginner and intermediate parenting levels and feel you're ready for expert level.

Once your teen is back on their feet, which may be days, or even weeks, after their stupid mistake has occurred, shift your role into being the coach who helps them figure out how to avoid making the same mistake again. Be as diplomatic as possible in walking them through a post-mortem of what went wrong and help them figure out how to do better next time. Ask leading questions, rather than volunteering your own opinions. For instance:

- What do you think caused you to get into this situation?
- Do you think this happened because of something you did, or was it something outside of your control?
- What do you think you can do differently next time so that it doesn't happen again?

Once you've discussed how to avoid making the same mistake again… never speak of it again. Unless it looks like they're about to make that same mistake a second time, in which case, give them a gentle—or not so gentle—reminder.

Remember that the ultimate goal of letting your teen make some stupid mistakes is for them to take responsibility for their mistakes and learn something from them so they can avoid finding themselves in similar situations in the future. Give your teen the opportunity to learn from their own mistakes, as long as the long-term consequences of those mistakes aren't too severe.

"Children are apt to live up to what you believe of them."

–Lady Bird Johnson

DAD'S GREAT ADVICE
FOR
PARENTS OF TEENS #22

MAKE SEX MATTER-OF-FACT

*Model a healthy and open "sex positive"
attitude, but do so in a way that
doesn't scar your teen for life.*

Are you sitting down? This piece of Great Advice is going to be
R-rated for mature audiences only, so prepare yourself... it might
be a tough one for some parents to take. In fact, if you haven't
reached the ultra-advanced level of parenting yet, you might want
to sit this one out and just move on to the next piece of Great
Advice.

In many, many countries and cultures in this world, sex is
treated as a taboo subject, which is just a bit ironic, given that all
eight billion of us owe our lives to sex. It's fair to say that most
people agree that sex is something that should generally be done
in private, behind closed doors, but that doesn't mean it should
only be discussed in private and behind closed doors (quite the
opposite, in fact). Doing so only teaches our kids that it's a taboo
subject to discuss. Combine this with the fact that teens constantly
feel pressure to not have sex until they're older, and they get the
message that it's not just a taboo subject, but a taboo action. And
that's... not good.

Instead, the goal should be an approach that's now commonly

referred to as "sex positivity." Being "sex positive" generally means abandoning the cultural attitudes and norms around treating sex as something shameful or something to be embarrassed about, and recognizing sex as a natural part of being a human being. Said differently, "sex positivity" aims to treat consensual sexual activity as a basic, healthy, pleasurable activity that we can all talk about openly in a matter-of-fact manner without embarrassment, judgment, or fear.

And so, if you're aiming to raise your teen in a "sex positive" manner, sex should be discussed openly and without shame or embarrassment in your home. For many parents, that's a hard pill to swallow. However, I guarantee that sex is being discussed a lot among teenagers at school and at any social gathering they attend. I also guarantee that you probably don't want your teen's entire sexual knowledge to come from another completely oblivious teen. Talk about the blind leading the blind! Hearing a teen say, "You can't get pregnant if it's your first time," is enough to make any parent throw their hands up in exasperation.

So you want to create a sex-positive atmosphere at home, where sex and healthy relationships are openly discussed, talked about, joked about, and even on display.

"On display?! Are you suggesting we should have sex in front of our kids?!"

Uh… only if you want your kid to spend the next fifty years in therapy. Unless you want your teenager to be scarred for life, do not have sex in front of your kid. (Heck, even if you DO want your teenager to be scarred for life, just yell "I love you" to them every time you drop them off at school, and that should do the trick.) However, there's no need to hide your (hopefully) healthy, romantic relationship with your partner from your teen either. It's OK to start having more adult conversations around your teens, and adults sometimes drop sexual talk into conversation.

An easy place to start is by not shying away from sexually-themed jokes. Extra credit if you use a sexually-themed "dad joke" like: "Having sex in an elevator is wrong on so many levels," or "69% of people find something dirty in every sentence."

It's a fine line, but it's important to do your best to avoid making any *personal* sexually-themed comments. For example, when the family is watching a movie together and a steamy scene pops up, instead of sitting there in awkward silence while everybody avoids eye contact, it's OK to comment to your partner with the teens in earshot, "I didn't even realize that position was possible." In contrast, it's probably not OK to shout, "Hey honey, I think we've got this couple beat for sure!" We're trying to help our kids, not hurt them.

If some suggestive talk doesn't take you too far out of your comfort zone, then take things to the next "sex positive" level and make a habit of kissing your partner in front of your teen. Heck, you can even have a mini make-out session in full public view from time to time. Will it disgust your teen enough to make them throw up? Likely, yes. But they're seeing the same make-out sessions on TV and between kids in the hallway at school, so it won't be anything new for them. Plus, instead of seeing two people making out in public, each of whom (given the way high schoolers work) will very likely be making out with a different person next week, at least this is a make-out session between two people in a long-term committed relationship. So start the make-out sesh! Again, though, don't take it too far. Save the tongues for the bedroom, please. It's OK to disgust your teen, but let's not kill them.

A good guideline about where the line should be drawn is that your kids should know their parents are still in a healthy sexual relationship, but without knowing all the details. For instance, if you're only having sex when your kid is out of the house, you're hiding something you shouldn't be ashamed of. It's fine for them to see a locked bedroom door every so often, even if they're old enough now where they can figure out what's going on behind it. Just keep the noise to a minimum, please. Again, we don't want to cause any permanent damage to our teens.

Don't bring your teen up thinking that sex is shameful or embarrassing or something never to be discussed with their friends. Model a healthy and open "sex positive" attitude, but do so in a way that doesn't scar your teen for life.

"Modeling a healthy marriage is one of the best gifts you can give your child."

–Dr. Gary Chapman

GET THEM HELP IF THEY NEED IT

If your teen has a big problem, stop reading books and get them professional help.

I'm quite proud of the *Dad's Great Advice* book series, primarily because the books have helped thousands of teens, parents of teens, and others. The Great Advice in these books helps people solve some of their most pressing problems and issues and leads them toward living happier lives.

However, I hope it's clear that the problems and issues addressed in this book (and others in the series) and the Great Advice given to address those problems and issues are aimed at a very wide audience. That is, they're the types of problems and issues that most of us experience, and that are "small" enough problems and issues that we can hope to fix them ourselves with a little hard work, determination, and discipline.

But as you might know, sometimes "small" problems lead to "big" problems. And the greatest Great Advice, the greatest parenting, and the greatest care and attention you give your teen sometimes just aren't great enough to shelter them from having big problems.

Sadly, there are lots and lots of teens who have big problems in their life, bigger problems than any teenager should have to face.

Problems like eating disorders, learning disabilities, addiction, suicidal thoughts, physical abuse, sexual abuse, mental health issues, low self-esteem, bullying, self-harm, and other serious issues.

Parents want to see their teen in the best light possible and, as a result, some parents tend to miss or even ignore some of the warning signs that teens display when they have big problems. Some parents recognize warning signs, but are afraid to admit to themselves that their teen might have some really big problems they're dealing with. And some parents recognize that their teen has some big problems, but think that they can help their teen work through those problems themselves.

If one of your teen's small problems has turned into a big problem, I hope it's obvious to you that the Great Advice in a book from a dad who doesn't personally know your teen and their problems isn't great enough to help. Similarly, even the Great Advice from you, your teen's own parent—someone who is probably amazingly intelligent, kind, and empathetic, and who knows their teen's problems firsthand—might not be great enough to help either.

If your teen has a big problem, you should get them help from a professional therapist, who not only can get to know your teen and their problems personally, but also has a lot more experience than you do in how to effectively help your teen with their big problems.

When it comes to parenting teens, sometimes you have to admit when you need some professional help.

If you think there's still a social stigma in a teenager seeing a therapist like there may have been when you were a teen, think again. If you get your teen professional help for their problem, they will be in good company: about 17% of teenagers have received some sort of mental health treatment.

Money shouldn't get in the way of getting your teen professional help either. While it's true that many mental health professionals are very expensive and aren't covered by insurance, there are a myriad of free and inexpensive options available in most communities. You just have to ask around and be aggressive to find those affordable options sometimes.

How do you know when a small problem for your teen has turned into a big problem? Sometimes it's obvious. Often times it's not. Because the stakes are so high, the best strategy is to simply err on the side of caution and, if you suspect your teen might be facing a big problem, speak with a professional about it, whether your teen agrees to come with you to discuss things or not.

If your teen has a big problem, stop reading books and get them professional help.

"Ask for help. Not because you are weak. But because you want to remain strong."

–Les Brown

CHOOSE YOUR BATTLES WISELY

Give in on the smaller things and save the battles for the really important issues.

"Choose your battles with your teen wisely"—well, unfortunately, that's much easier said than done. There are no rules, so your decisions in choosing your battles have to be made on a case-by-case basis, in the heat of the moment, when emotions and tensions are high.

Remember that if you choose your battles wisely, when you do finally stand your ground and put your foot down, it will have a lot more impact than it would if you complain about and push back on every little thing.

While it's hard to identify the battles with your teen that are definitely worth choosing, it's much easier to identify the battles that are not worth fighting. Here are some easy battles you can let them win (and a few that might be worth pushing back on):

1. **Personal Appearance (Hair/Makeup)**
   When your little baby was a little baby, you might not have envisioned them with a purple mohawk and black eyeliner, but if that's how they envision themselves, you might want to go with it. Personal appearance is, well…

personal. Rather than fight back against the person they see themselves to be, try embracing that person, even if it's not the person YOU see them to be.

BATTLES THAT MAY BE WORTH FIGHTING:
Draw the line at supporting permanent body modifications like tattoos and body piercings, because a fifteen-year-old might regret having that face tattoo when they're twenty. If need be, negotiate with them: Offer to pay for their tattoo or piercing if they still want it when they turn eighteen (because they're going to do what they want at eighteen anyway).

2. **Clothing**
   In general, let your teens wear what they want to wear. Along with their hair and makeup, their clothes are part of how they express themselves, and it's generally a good idea to let your kid express themselves in the way they see fit. For the most part, this means not commenting when clothing seems too sexually suggestive for your tastes. It's fair to have conversations with your teen about what their clothes and the way they dress say about them as a person and about how they view themselves, but if they're comfortable with it, just bite your lip, support them, and let school dress codes do the dirty work for you.

   BATTLES THAT MAY BE WORTH FIGHTING:
   When clothing goes to the extreme, it might be time to put your foot down. Clothing with offensive or violent messages, or clothing that is way past the point of being inappropriate or sexually provocative, is worthy of putting your foot down and opening up a longer discussion.

3. Messy Bedroom
Let their bedroom be their space. Let them keep it as messy as they'd like, within reason, as long as it doesn't impinge upon other members of your family. This is one of the easiest battles to let them win. All you have to do is keep the door shut and never look inside (and try to ignore any stench wafting out into the hallway).

BATTLES THAT MAY BE WORTH FIGHTING:
Definitely put your foot down when it comes to food messes. Moldy, rotting food is going to cause problems with smells and insects and other critters, so strike a deal: If they agree to keep their room clean of food and other potential hazards, you'll let them manage their room as they see fit. Also, the mess must remain in their room. They're still responsible for cleaning up after themselves in common areas of the home.

4. Conversations
So they don't like to talk. Don't make them. Let them be as antisocial as they like. Push them a little to join the conversation, but not a lot. Keep the lines of communication open so that they know that you're always open to chatting if they ever feel like it. (See *Dad's Great Advice for Parents of Teens #10*, "Become a Conversational Ninja," in this book.)

BATTLES THAT MAY BE WORTH FIGHTING:
Don't allow them to speak or act disrespectfully to you or anybody else.

5. **Unhealthy Eating**

The best, easiest time to teach your child to eat healthy is before they hit their teen years. The worst, hardest time to do so is during their teen years. Make sure that there is always healthy food in the house that is easily accessible to your teen if they want it, but if they choose to eat crap instead of the good stuff, don't get on their case about it.

BATTLES THAT MAY BE WORTH FIGHTING:
If their weight is becoming unhealthy, it's imperative that you discuss it, and get them help from a professional if necessary so they can remain healthy. Just be very careful how you do it, because eating disorders and body image issues can become serious issues for teens.

6. **Homework**

It's OK to stay on your teen to make sure their home-work is getting done, but don't dictate when, how, and where it gets done. Offer to help them manage their time and reduce procrastination if they're open to it. If they're not, allow them to handle their homework themselves and demonstrate that they're on top of it.

BATTLES THAT MAY BE WORTH FIGHTING:
If their grades drop, or if they're not putting in the effort to at least try to succeed, then it may be time to step in and set some guidelines around how they study and how much they study.

7. **Social Media Usage**

There are many, many teens who spend way, way too much time on social media. However, it's really tough to reign in social media usage once the genie is out of the bottle. Setting time limits or using apps or software like Apple's Screen Time can help, but there are so many ways a clever teen can sidetrack those methods that trying to limit their time on social media can be a futile endeavor. You probably don't want to be in the business of watching over them constantly and fighting over whether they've spent enough time on social media for one day.

BATTLES THAT MAY BE WORTH FIGHTING:
Having a "bedtime" for their phone each night and a separate place to charge their phone outside of the bedroom are somewhat effective and reasonable ways of limiting social media usage. Also, make it mandatory that they accept you as a follower for each of their social media accounts, and if you ever see them post something that crosses the line into inappropriate or dangerous behavior, make sure you address it immediately.

In general, most day-to-day battles are best left unfought. The ones that are worth fighting are the biggies that concern their health and safety: drinking, vaping, drug use, sexual activity, bullying, and violence, to name a few. Those are battles worth fighting in the sense that they deserve some major discussion.

One other major area that is a battle worth fighting: Lying. Trusting your teen, and making them earn your trust, is key to building a strong relationship with them. Make sure they know that honesty is non-negotiable, and while you're willing to give in when it comes to many other battles, lying is not one of them.

Overall, just remember that, in any battle, diplomacy should be your first tactic, not all out war. And for good reason! If you do battle on some of these fronts, and you deliver ultimatums on what your teen can and can't do, they might figure out that they CAN actually get away with doing these things behind your back.

And when you catch them, you'll punish them, which will piss them off even more, and cause what's known as a "major escalation in hostilities," which can lead to what's known as "mutually assured destruction" which, as you might be able to tell from the phrasing, ain't good. So whenever possible, opt for diplomacy and negotiation with your teen.

Don't fight with your teen about every little disagreement. Give in on the smaller things and save the battles for the really important issues.

"You don't have to show up to every argument you're invited to."

–Unknown

BE GRATEFUL FOR THEM

We could all use some improvement, but make sure you take a moment each day to appreciate how great your teen is just as they are.

There's a popular story that's been going around the internet for years about parents who found a note on their teenager's pillow one morning. The note said something like this:

"Dear Mom and Dad, I decided last night that I need to leave home, so I took the car. I was going to take Mom's car, but I dented the bumper pulling out of the driveway, so I took Dad's car instead. I needed a car because I'm moving out west where Jim lives. Jim and I have been secretly dating for seven months, because I didn't think you'd approve of me dating a fifty-year-old man, especially not one with two kids of his own. But we're in love, and I want to share my life with him, and that life needs to be where Jim has his job delivering pizzas, because we need the security of that job, not just to pay for our wedding next week, but also because I'm three months pregnant. With Jim's twins. And we want to save up enough money so we can move out of Jim's van and into an apartment before the babies come. I know this is a shock, but I hope you can be happy for me. And I'm confident you will be happy for me once you learn that everything in this letter was a lie. Except for me denting the car, which hopefully seems like no big deal now, given how bad things could have been. Love, Me."

Regardless of whether or not a brilliant kid actually wrote that letter in real life, it makes a great point to all parents:

Don't sweat the small stuff, and be grateful if there is no big stuff.

I'm going out on a limb here, but I'm guessing that you and your teen are probably both human beings. And as human beings, it's a certainty that you're not yet perfect, and have room for improvement in many different areas of your life. And especially when reading a book of Great Advice to help you improve your parenting and your teen's life, it's easy to get hyper-focused on all the areas that you and your teen are falling short and missing the mark.

Even though there are lots of things you and your teen could do to be happier and make your life better, make sure you keep things in perspective. Make sure you take time to appreciate and be grateful for all the great things about your teen. Because, just as the parent who received the letter above probably discovered, if your teen isn't in the hospital, or in prison, or married, or a teen parent, then, in the grand scheme of things, you should count yourself lucky. A dented car, bad grades, broken curfews, and mean friends aren't things that any parent wishes for, but if those are the biggest issues that your teen brings home with them, keep things in perspective and realize that those things aren't really that awful.

And what if there is some big stuff going on in your teen's life? What if your teen actually is a teen parent, or married, or in prison, or worst of all, in the hospital?

Actually, the same Great Advice applies to you. Even if there's some really crappy things going on in your teen's life, make sure you take a moment every now and then to be grateful for whatever it is in your teen's life that is going well, and thankful for whatever time you get to enjoy with your teen each day. No human being is perfect, but every human being (even one who is far from perfect) has something you can be grateful for. Every once in a while, take a few minutes to focus on all the great things that make your teen unique and special and all the things they do that bring happiness and joy into your life.

We could all use some improvement, but make sure you take a moment each day to appreciate how great your teen is just as they are.

"The most precious jewels you'll ever have around your neck are the arms of your children."

–Unknown

A WARNING ABOUT GREAT ADVICE

Reading about Great Advice isn't really all that valuable if you don't eventually put some of that Great Advice to use. It's one thing to read about becoming a better parent to your teen, but it's another thing entirely to actually *become* a better parent to your teen. In other words...

Now that you've read this book, try to live it.

But I must warn you before you do: It could be overwhelming to try to put all the Great Advice in this book, or even just some of it, into effect. Reading about Great Advice is easy, but putting even one of these pieces of Great Advice into effect is hard. Really hard. The good news is that I developed something that can help you.

For each piece of Great Advice in this book, I developed a short checklist of a few simple challenges that will help you put the Great Advice into effect. This "Challenge Checklist" includes some simple tasks you can do (usually in less than five minutes) to immediately see the benefits of putting the Great Advice to work for you. Some of the challenges are difficult, some are easy, some are scary, and some are simply thought-provoking.

The *Dad's Great Advice for Parents of Teens: Challenge Checklist* is included with the purchase of this book, so you can download it for free here:

greatadvicegroup.com/checklist6

161

If you want to get the most value out of this book, and want a bit of help in translating the Great Advice into action, please make sure to download the free *Challenge Checklist* to help you get started.

P.S. Keep reading! More Great Advice from other books appears in the "Bonus Advice" section that follows.

Bonus Great Advice

More Great Advice from Other Books in the *Dad's Great Advice* Series

There are many more pieces of Great Advice from other books in the *Dad's Great Advice* series that are relevant to you as the parent of a teen. Some of them apply directly to you as a parent, others apply more indirectly as Great Advice for you to give to your teen. While there were a lot to choose from, I've included ten of the best here in this Bonus Advice section. Enjoy!

The Great Advice in this section is taken from the following *Dad's Great Advice* books:

Dad's Great Advice for Teens
Dad's Great Advice for College Students
Dad's Great Advice for All Parents
Dad's Great Advice About Life Skills for Teens
Dad's Great Advice for Everyone

FIND BALANCE IN YOUR PARENTING

*Adopt an "authoritative parenting" style by
demanding a lot from your child, but also
by being incredibly supportive of them.*

Your parents had their own personal style in everything they did. It was probably an awful, ugly, old-fashioned style, but style it was. They wore tacky clothes, had embarrassing hairstyles, listened to lame music, and used out-of-touch phrases that weren't quite as on fleek as the fierce phrases we flex today.

Your parents had their own parenting style too. Chances are you'll probably adopt something similar to their parenting style with your own child. Before you do, though, you should give some thought to exactly what you want your parenting style to be, because it can have a pretty big effect on your kid.

"Parenting style" isn't just some casual phrase we use to refer to how you parent. It's a well-defined term that psychologists use to represent a set of standard strategies that parents use with their kids. To over-simplify things, parenting style refers to how responsive a parent is to their kid's needs, and how demanding they are of their children. To over-simplify things even more, it refers to how supportive and how strict a parent is.

Back in "the old days," lots of parents weren't very responsive to their kid's needs, and were pretty darn strict and demanding, especially when it came to schoolwork and achievement. The thinking was that kids should follow the rules without question, be obedient and listen to their parents, and be punished harshly when breaking the rules. Parents weren't interested in getting feedback from their kids about the rules, and when kids asked their parents why the rule had to be that way, the standard refrain was, "Because I said so!"

This kind of parenting style is called "authoritarian parenting," and it's pretty obvious why that name was chosen. The parent runs the show, and so this "my way or the highway" attitude is a great parenting style... if you're the parent. But as you might expect, this parenting style isn't so great for kids. It often results in stressed out, aggressive kids with low self-esteem.

More recently, we've seen a parenting style that swings far the other way. Parents who adopt this style are very responsive to their kid's feelings and needs, and not very demanding of them at all. That is, they're extremely lenient, don't set many rules, and rarely punish their kids. They try to interfere in their kid's life as little as possible, and act in the role of a friend more than the role of a parent.

This kind of parenting style is called "permissive parenting," and again, it's pretty obvious why that name was chosen. The kid runs the show in this parenting style, which has many benefits at first glance. The parents get relieved of many of the responsibilities of being a parent—which, as a parent, sounds like a really nice, long vacation—and the kid essentially gets treated as if they were an adult, which, as a kid, sounds like paradise. Everybody wins! It's the perfect parenting style! Except for one small, tiny, itsy-bitsy problem: kids aren't actually adults, they're just kids. (That's actually why Merriam-Webster's has separate words for each of them.) Kids that are raised using this permissive parenting style may enjoy their freedom, but they often lack self-control, struggle academically, and exhibit more behavioral problems.

So if authoritarian parenting is too strict and harsh, and permissive parenting doesn't demand enough of your child, what should you be aiming for?

Balance. A little bit of both.

You want to be demanding enough of your kid that they have rules to follow, but responsive enough that they feel like they have input on the rules and that their feelings are respected. You want to be supportive of them, but set expectations of them as well. You want to give them unconditional love, but keep challenging them and holding them to a high standard.

This style of parenting is called "authoritative parenting" (which sounds a lot like authoritarian parenting, but couldn't be more different), and psychologists generally agree that this is what you should be aiming for. Kids raised using this style are generally happier and make better decisions.

What types of things should you do to become an authoritative parent?

- Set high expectations of your child to act in a mature way, but when they fall short of the goal, be forgiving and understanding of their shortcomings.
- Set rules for them and explain your rationale in setting those rules. Then entertain and listen sincerely to their objections and rebuttals to those rules. Since kids aren't typically as logical and rational as adults (we'd like to think), nobody says you have to adjust the rules because of your child's objections, the important thing is to listen to them and address them. And of course, from time to time, unless you're one of those perfect parents who never makes

a mistake, they might actually have a valid rebuttal to your ill-conceived rule forbidding any mention of Taylor Swift at the dinner table, and you'll want to actually address their objections. Doing so empowers your kid to feel like they're respected, listened to, and being treated fairly.

- When your kid misbehaves, instead of punishing your child, take the time to discuss why what they did was wrong and why they shouldn't do it again. This will teach them not to misbehave because that particular behavior is wrong, not just because they want to avoid the punishment. Does it take a lot more time and effort than a quick punishment or "time out"? Yes. But it's truly worth taking the time.

You might notice that, even with an authoritative parenting style, the parent still makes the decisions, and therefore you might say they're still acting as an authoritarian. That's true, but there's a very big difference between simply dictating the rules all the time as an authoritarian, and taking feedback and input from your kid, considering it, and then dictating the rules. The very big difference is that, in the latter case, your child feels empowered with a sense of independence and autonomy, and in the former scenario, they just feel bossed around and dream of the day when they can overthrow the authoritarian. (And someday, overthrow the authoritarian they will.)

So authoritative parenting should be your goal, but if becoming one sounds hard, don't fret. There's a very simple shortcut you can take that will force you to become an authoritative parent almost overnight: Write a note to your child that reads, "Whenever we are discussing something, I promise to never, ever use the phrase 'Because I said so.'" Sign that note, hand it over to your child, and then honor it. I can assure you that doing so will make your life significantly harder and more annoying, but one day, years from now, you'll be glad you did it.

Adopt an authoritative parenting style by demanding a lot from your child, but also by being incredibly supportive of them.

"Parenting style: Somewhere between 'No, don't do that!' and 'Oh, whatever.'"

–Unknown

FIGURE OUT HOW TO
BE SUCCESSFUL

Figure out for yourself what it means to be successful, and remember that the things that make other people feel successful might not be the same things that make you feel successful.

If I were to ask you who the most successful people in the world are, what names first come to mind? The most popular answers I get to this question are Bill Gates, Jeff Bezos, and Warren Buffett.

Why do those people keep coming up more than any other? After all, there are lots of successful business people in the world who have built really successful companies that are helping lots of people live better lives. So why those three? The answer is probably obvious: money.

Those three people happen to be among the richest people in the world. They're at the top of the top of what we call "the 1 percent." And the way most people measure somebody's success is by how much money they have.

Here's the interesting thing though. If you're making more than about $32,000 a year, you are part of the 1 percent too. To be specific, you're part of the top 1 percent of income earners in the world. That means you're earning more than eight billion other people. So does this make you feel successful? And if you're not making more than $32,000 a year, does that make you feel unsuccessful?

Maybe. Maybe not. But regardless, is money the only way of measuring success? Is money the best way of measuring success?

No, it isn't.

In fact, the best metric to measure success is not the amount of money you have, but rather, it's the amount of happiness you have. Happiness is the one thing we're all trying to maximize. Now it just so happens that most people believe the biggest driver of their happiness is how much money they have. But is it actually true that money really does drive happiness?

As it turns out, it isn't true. Money is not the biggest driver of happiness. Not by a longshot.

In the most recent rankings of the richest countries of the world, Qatar was ranked the highest in per capita income. But you may be surprised to learn that Qatar is only ranked 29th when it comes to happiness. On the other hand, Finland is ranked all the way down at number 24 when it comes to average per capita income. But Finland is also ranked as the happiest country in the world. So why isn't the richest country the happiest, and why isn't the happiest country the richest? (And more curiously, why is Finland so happy when they're also so cold?)

Even though most people directly tie money to happiness and success, when they are pressed on the issue, most of them quickly realize this isn't true. Don't believe me? I'm going to make you a deal, and I'd like to know if you would accept the offer.

I'll snap my fingers and make you an instant billionaire. You will have all the money you will ever need, a beautiful house, a huge yacht, a private jet, and most importantly, the latest iPhone. But... in the process, you'll lose contact with all your current friends, your spouse or significant other, your parents, your brothers and sisters, and your extended family members. You'll have all the money you want but you'll have no loved ones to share it with. Is that success to you?

I'm guessing it's not. And I'm guessing it's not because I happen to know that a lot of people who have a huge bank account, a huge house, and a huge yacht, also have huge therapy bills. And they have huge therapy bills because they realized, perhaps a bit too late, that their success wasn't only driven by money, and that they may have dropped the ball in other areas of their life in which they also measure their success and happiness.

There are lots of other ways to define success, other than how much money you have. One of the best illustrations of this I've heard is a story that my good friend Archimedes Clutterbuck told me the last time he went skiing. He took a lesson with a ski instructor who had been doing his job more than forty years. The instructor lived a pretty spartan, frugal life, living out of his van most of the year. But he also told Archimedes, "I'd rather live out of my van and ski every day out in nature than make ten times more money and be stuck inside at a desk all day." He measured his success not by how much money was in his bank account, or how big a house he lived in, but by how many days a year he was able to ski.

The things that make your friends think you're successful, the things that make your parents think you're successful, and the things that make your colleagues think you're successful, might not be the same things that make YOU feel successful. You're responsible for figuring out for yourself the things that will make you feel successful and the things that will bring you happiness.

And there are a huge variety of things that you might use to determine how successful you are: how many days you get to ski, how many close friends you have, how many people you make laugh, how many kids you have, how many countries you visit, how much time you spend with your significant other, how many lives you save, how many trees you plant, or how many people you feed.

So don't assume that money is the best measure of your success and happiness, because it probably isn't. Figure out for yourself what it means for you to be successful.

"Don't measure your success with someone else's ruler."

–Unknown

DON'T BELIEVE A WORD YOUR BOYFRIEND/GIRLFRIEND SAYS

When trying to figure out how "into you" your boyfriend/girlfriend is, put more weight on what they do, than what they say.

There are many honest people in this world who say exactly what they mean and, for better or worse, will truly express how they feel about their significant other. The world needs as many of these people as possible.

And yet, there are others who are not so honest and forthright—people who are, to use a technical term, jerks.

There's a well-known stereotype out there about the male gender that goes something like this: "Guys only have one thing on their minds." Naturally, that one thing is... Taco Bell.

OK, it's not Taco Bell. The one thing they're referring to on every guy's mind is... sex (or any kind of sexual experience), although Taco Bell might run a close second.

Like all stereotypes, it's unfair to apply this to everyone. There are a lot of guys out there who don't have a one-track mind. And conversely, there are a lot of girls who, like some guys, only have that same thing on their minds too.

Whether a guy or a girl, having sex in their thoughts isn't, in itself, a bad thing. Every single one of the 7.8 billion people on this planet owe their existence to sex, and almost every single one of those 7.8 billion people will have some sort of sexual experience before they leave this planet. And because there are approximately 7.8 billion people having sex, whoever invented sex way back when made sure that it was a fun, enjoyable experience.

The fact that many guys and girls often seem to have sex on their mind isn't the problem. The real problem is that when sex is the only thing on somebody's mind, a person tends to say anything they need to say to convince somebody else to satisfy that amazingly strong human desire, whether it's true or not. They might say things like, "I love you so much," or "I want to be in a committed relationship and only date you," or "I really care a lot about you," when it doesn't really reflect their true feelings.

Now some people really mean it when they say those things. But some don't. So how do you know which type of person you're talking to? How can you tell the person that really means the beautiful things they say, from the person that doesn't? How can you tell the person who really cares about you from the person who really only cares about fooling around with you?

It's actually quite simple: Don't listen to what they say; watch what they do.

Here are some things that people DO that demonstrate they might not like you as much as you think they do:

- They say they're going to do something with you, but then cancel or don't follow through.
- They always have to have things their way, rarely giving in or compromising.
- They ask for lots of favors, but don't do many favors for you.
- They only make plans with you at the last minute, when they don't have anything else to do.

- They disrespect you by saying mean things or calling you names.
- They don't call or text you that often.
- They don't ask questions about you.
- They don't take interest in the things you're interested in.
- They don't introduce you to their friends, or don't pay attention to you when their friends are around.
- They often can't find time to be with you because they're too busy.

On the other hand, here are some things that people DO that demonstrate that they probably really like you:

- They do the things they say they're going to do.
- They often give in and compromise.
- They do favors for you when you ask.
- They make plans with you days or weeks in advance.
- They say nice things to you, and say nice things about you.
- They call and text you often.
- They ask a lot of questions about you, and about what's going on in your life.
- They take interest in the things you're interested in, even if those things don't interest them.
- They introduce you to their friends, and pay close attention to you when their friends are around.
- They try to spend a lot of time with you, even if they're busy.
- They try to do things that make you happy, and try to avoid doing things that make you unhappy.

You'll notice a common theme among most of the items above: They all take a lot of time.

Somebody that really cares about you wants to spend time with you, and wants to spend time doing things that make you happy. Somebody that doesn't really care about you, has an easy time saying nice things (which doesn't take that much time), but has difficulty spending the time that it takes to demonstrate that they really care about you.

In short, a jerk will say anything they can to get what they want, because it's quick and easy to fake. But they won't usually DO the things that show they care, because it takes a lot more time to fake that.

If you're questioning somebody's feelings for you, ignore all the things they say, and pay attention to all the things they do.

"Actions speak louder than words."

–Proverb

DON'T HAVE TOO MANY FRIENDS

*Don't worry so much about how many friends
you have. When it comes to friendship,
it's all about quality, not quantity.*

In our society, it seems like we're taught that more is always better. More money, more cars, more possessions, more power, more status, more everything! Obviously though, it's not exactly true, or even close to true. One area in particular where this rule doesn't apply is when it comes to friendships.

With friendships, more does not mean better.

Lots of people aspire to be popular. Popular people have plenty of friends and admirers who want to spend time with them. It's like being a bit of a local celebrity. As a result, people often go out of their way to accumulate a lot of friends. Even our social media tracks how many "friends" or "followers" we have, even though most of them can't really be considered friends at all, just acquaintances, if that.

Creating new friendships is obviously a really good thing to do. And it seems like the more friendships we create, the better. Especially in college, where the opportunities to meet new people and create friendships are ten times more abundant than what you experience in the "real world," you might feel so overwhelmed and excited by all the new people you meet that you end up trying to maintain every single one of those friendships. In short, you feel like you want to be friends with everyone you meet.

However, there's a big problem with having a lot of friends. You end up spreading yourself really, really thin. It takes a lot of time and effort to keep up with friendships, and the more friendships you try to keep up with, the more time and effort it takes. As a result, you end up with lots and lots of friends, but no close friends.

And close friends are what life is all about. Close friends are the ultimate goal.

Close friends are something more than just a friend. So much more. They make you a better person. They support you when times get tough. They listen to you. They're honest with you (whether you're right or wrong). They always have your back (whether you're right or wrong). They make you laugh. They make you feel better. They help you live longer. They help you chill out. They keep you humble. They forgive you. They trust you. They truly care about you.

It's not easy to find a close friend. In fact, if you're lucky enough to find even two or three close friends in your lifetime, I think you're doing pretty darn well. It's a challenge to find a close friend primarily because of all the time it takes to find someone you really connect with, and to build enough trust with them to move the friendship to the next level.

In fact, scientists have studied friendship and figured out about how long it takes to develop a friend and a close friend. The short answer: a lot of time. They found that it takes, on average, 164 hours of time together for an acquaintance to become a friend. And to make a good friend, it takes, on average, 219 hours spent together! Obviously, the more people you're acquaintances or friends with, the harder it is to spend the 219 hours it takes to really connect and bond to create a "close friend."

I should be clear that having some close friends doesn't preclude you from having lots of other friends. The key is to make sure that you're spending extra time—quality, meaningful time—with your close friends. Because if you're trying to connect closely with too many people at once, you end up not connecting closely with anybody at all. In other words, finding and developing close friends is a matter of depth over breadth. Quality over quantity.

Don't worry so much about how many friends you have. Focus on developing your relationships with your close friends by spending quality time with them.

"Wishing to be friends is quick work, but friendship is a slow ripening fruit."

–Aristotle

DAD'S GREAT ADVICE
FOR
TEENS #15

DON'T TRUST YOUR BRAIN
TO MAKE DECISIONS

Trust your gut. Even though we don't yet know how or why, sometimes your intuition is smarter than your brain.

If you look back at all the crazy things people thought were true just a few hundred years ago, those people look like idiots. They used to think drinking mercury was good for you. (It's not. It will kill you.) They used to think bloodletting using leeches was a good idea to get rid of infections. (It isn't. It's disgusting.) They used to think the world is flat. (It isn't. But some people still aren't convinced.)

Of course, this means that we're all going to look like idiots to the people of the future. "Those dolts didn't even know how to levitate!" they'll say.

One of the crazier things scientists recently discovered may be true is that the idea of "trusting your gut" to help you make decisions actually works. They've discovered that our human bodies and other living creatures are capable of sensing things we don't even realize we're sensing. The human body really does have something called "intuition" or a "gut feeling," and it ends up being right significantly more than 50 percent of the time. Our bodies are capable of knowing some things that we don't consciously know ourselves.

Unfortunately, these scientists don't yet know how this happens, but thankfully, we don't really need to know how it happens to use this little superpower of ours. And so my Great Advice to you is...

Always trust your gut.

Understand and accept that, somehow, your brain and body are working on levels that you can't consciously understand, but can feel nevertheless. So learn to feel it. Learn to feel your gut. And more importantly, learn to trust your gut. It's usually right.

It can be frustrating to hear "trust your gut" if you don't think you can feel your "gut" or "intuition." Admittedly, it's hard to get in touch with your gut, especially as a teen. It's not something that happens overnight, but here's one tactic you can use that has worked for me.

Let's say you're faced with a decision of whether to join the school play or the tennis team (you can't do both). You're likely to do some sort of informal list of pros and cons for each option, and then use that list to help make your decision. If that works for you, great. But if you make your little list of pros and cons and still feel like things are evenly balanced, then you have to defer to your gut. Here's how to do it:

Flip a coin.

Heads means you do the school play, tails means you join the tennis team. Decide ahead of time that you're going to commit to whatever it is that fate decides for you. Then when you flip that coin and look at the result, take stock of the immediate feeling you get. If you get a reaction of relief and happiness, then follow the coin. But if you look at the coin and think, *Best out of three?* that's your gut speaking to you. Listen to your gut and tell that stupid coin to go jump in a lake.

Listening to your gut is easier said than done, I know. But it's also a skill you can get better at. Years ago, my good friend Archimedes Clutterbuck got into a very prestigious college, as well as a smaller college that he applied to just because the campus felt right. He turned down the prestigious college for the one that felt right to his gut, and never regretted his decision.

Later in life, Archie had to hire a graphic designer to create a logo. One candidate had years of experience, while another, though less experienced, seemed to click with Archie creatively. Against his gut, he chose the more experienced person, and ended up getting a terrible result and regretting it. He later hired the more inexperienced person and got a logo that he loved.

As you try to listen to your gut more, you'll get better at hearing it and following it. And when you do, you'll probably start to notice some amazing results. In fact, I recommend you try a little experiment.

Start keeping track of major decisions you make—particularly decisions where you really want to decide one thing, but because of logical evidence or other people's opinions, you are tempted to do another thing. Write down what your gut tells you to do, what your head tells you to do, and the decision you ultimately make.

Then once the decision plays itself out, be it days, weeks, or months later, ask yourself if things turned out well with that decision, or if you'd view the decision as a bad one.

I can tell you that, for the past few years, Archimedes has been tracking these times that his "gut" didn't necessarily agree with what his head was telling him. And I was amazed when he told me that, without exception, when he trusted his gut, things ended up moving in a positive direction. And without exception, when he ignored his gut and decided to trust his brain, things didn't go well. Pretty convincing stuff, huh?

So trust your gut. Listen to your intuition. Because even though we don't yet understand why or how, it seems certain that your gut is often smarter than your brain.

"Trust your instincts. Your intuition doesn't lie."

—Oprah Winfrey

SET FORMAL GOALS

Writing down and tracking your goals might be one of the most valuable life skills you ever learn.

I'm sure you have goals in your life. They might be big goals, like becoming a talented architect one day, or small goals, like beating the final boss in your favorite video game. If you're like most people, you spend a bit of time worrying about whether or not you're going to reach those goals.

What if I told you there was something you could do that would make it 42% more likely that you would reach your goal? I'm guessing you might reply that you don't want to expend all the extra time and effort it would take, even if it really were to increase your chances of reaching your goal by 42%. Fair enough.

But what if I told you that it would take you less than twenty seconds? Now would you do it?

It's not a joke. Science has shown that there's something you can do in less than twenty seconds that really will increase your chances of reaching your goal by 42%. All you have to do is simply...

Write down your goal.

So go ahead and write down one of your goals! I'll wait.

I know it seems crazy, but the simple act of writing your goals down increases your chances of achieving those goals for a bunch of reasons. The act of writing them down forces you to more clearly define exactly what it is you want to accomplish, it subtly motivates you more to work toward your goal, and it causes you to strategize about what your plan should be to attack your goal.

Writing down well-defined goals also helps in a lot of other areas, including self-confidence, responsibility, time management, resilience, perseverance, and developing a growth mindset.

Unfortunately, the opposite is also true. Without having any well-defined goals, you might find that your life simply becomes a thoughtless process of living one day to the next, without knowing where you're trying to get to or what you're trying to do over the long term.

So take some time to formalize the short-term and long-term goals you have, simply by writing them down. It's worth the time, and it's easy to do.

And if you're willing to write down your goals, maybe you're willing to take the next step and set better-defined goals in a more structured way. In fact, here's the crash course in how to do that in a super easy and fast way:

Crash Course in Goal-Setting

1. Write down one of your long-term goals.
2. Break down your long-term goal into smaller, shorter-term, more easily attainable sub-goals. Each sub-goal should be small enough that it can be accomplished in about a week.
3. Spend the week achieving that sub-goal.
4. Celebrate that you just got one week closer to your long-term goal!
5. Check in on your next sub-goal, and work toward that.
6. Repeat over and over until you get to the end of the long-term goal.

Congratulations! You just graduated from the Dad's Great Advice School of Goal-Setting. That's one less goal you have to achieve now.

And now, if you're interested in earning your advanced degree in goal-setting to get it just right, keep reading to learn about a more organized, methodical way.

Advanced Course in Goal-Setting

1. Core Values

Start your goal-setting by... ignoring your goals completely and listing out your core values, the very high-level things you care most about in the world that should drive your goals. Try to limit your core values to the five that are most important to you. If you focus on too many core values, then you end up prioritizing none of them.

There are lots of different core values that might be important to you, but here are some ideas you can choose from:

- Family, friendship, success, beauty, happiness, money, security, love, health, altruism, fame, creativity, status, honesty, kindness, leadership, accomplishment, intelligence, recognition, justice, respect, wisdom, fun.

2. Long-Term Goals

Write down some of the long-term goals you have. By "long-term" I mean goals you have that might take you ten to fifteen years to accomplish. These should be really big, lofty goals. Don't give too much thought to how realistic your long-term goals are, because almost any goal is realistic if you give yourself ten to fifteen years to achieve it. Plus, as you may learn one day, there are lots of people in this world who are going to try to convince you to give up on your goals and dreams, so the last thing you want to do is join in and quash your own goals just because it's going to take a lot of time and hard work to get there. What if a six-year-old Lionel Messi didn't set goals for himself in soccer because it was too unrealistic to become a professional soccer player?

If you need help figuring out what some of your long-term goals are, ask yourself these questions:

- What would you do if success was guaranteed?
- What does the life you envision for yourself fifteen years from now look like?
- What challenges do you face that, if you overcame them, would make you really proud?

Come up with one to three long-term goals in each of the following areas of your life:

- Work/Career
- Home/Family life
- Community/Society
- Self

Here are some examples of long-term goals:

"In fifteen years from now, I want to..."
- (Work/Career) Be a senior research biologist developing better vaccines
- (Home/Family Life) Be married with two children
- (Community/Society) Be a volunteer teacher at my local school
- (Self) Weigh 140 pounds and become a black-belt in karate

Whenever possible, make sure that your goals are as well-defined and as measurable as possible. For example, making your goal "Become a black-belt in karate" is better than "Get better at karate," and "Be a senior research biologist developing better vaccines" is better than "Be a scientist who helps discover things."

Once you choose your goals, write down the purpose of each goal, or why you chose that specific thing as your goal. Remembering the "why" behind each goal of yours helps keep you focused on your motivation toward that goal. Most purposes should include how that particular goal helps or serves other people in society, but if your goal doesn't happen to help other people, that's OK too.

EXAMPLES:

• I want to be a biologist so I can help discover a cure for an illness/condition.

• I want to volunteer as a teacher so I can help young kids get excited about learning new things.

Lastly, cross-reference your long-term goals with the core values you came up with earlier, and make sure that your goals match up with your core values. For example, if one of your core values is "Family" but one of your long-term goals in the Home/Family Life area is "Live alone in the wilderness for seven years," you might want to ask yourself if that is really the right goal for you, or conversely, if that really is one of your core values. There's nothing worse than working towards a goal for fifteen years only to figure out once you've achieved that goal that it's not really something you care about deep down inside.

3. **Short-Term Goals**

There's one big problem with having long-term goals set for ten to fifteen years from now: Those long-term goals aren't really that helpful in figuring out what you need to do on a daily, weekly, and monthly basis to reach them. But fear not. That's why we've got... short-term goals!

Take each of your long-term goals, and break those goals into smaller and smaller short-term goals. First, determine a realistic sub-goal of your long-term goal that you could realistically reach within the next year. Then once you have that year-long goal, break that down further into sub-goals you can accomplish in the first three months, the first month, and the first week.

For example, if your long-term goal is to become a black-belt in karate, a good goal for the next year might be to get your yellow belt in karate. Over the next month, as you work toward your yellow belt, a good goal might be to learn your first two karate forms. And over the next week, a good goal might be to learn the first two parts of the first karate form.

Again, make sure your short-term goals are as specific and measurable as possible, so it's absolutely clear if you achieved a goal or not. "Getting better" at karate is not a very measurable goal, and it will be hard to know the exact moment you achieve it. But "earning a yellow belt" is a very measurable goal, and you'll know you've achieved it the moment they place that yellow belt in your hands.

4. **Track Your Goals on a Regular Basis**

This could be the most important part of goal-setting. If you set a goal for yourself to achieve something by next year, but you don't think about that goal again until next year, there's a pretty good chance you're not going to reach that goal. Instead, put regular "goal check-ins" on your calendar to make sure you're making progress toward your yearly goal by achieving your quarterly, monthly, and weekly goals.

These check-ins don't need to take more than a minute or two. But make sure that you take time each week to remind yourself of your goal for the next week, and that you take time each month to remind yourself of the goal for the next month, etc.

Most importantly, when you do achieve one of your short-term goals, celebrate the small win! Because it's the small wins of achieving your goal for the week that keep you motivated and eventually add up to achieving your goal for the year.

I'll be honest with you: there are a lot of adults who go an entire lifetime without ever setting formal goals for themselves. And some of them probably reach some of their goals anyway. But everybody has goals they're trying to reach, and if the science is clear that the more formalized you are about setting and tracking your goals, the more likely you are to reach those goals, why wouldn't you spend the time to learn that skill and do it?

Writing down and tracking your goals might be one of the most valuable life skills you ever learn.

"People with goals succeed because they know where they're going."

–Earl Nightingale

TEACH THEM A GROWTH MINDSET

Teach your child to develop a growth mindset, which will help them realize that they're able to learn almost anything they set their mind to.

Not so many years ago, if your young kid did something wrong, the most common way to punish them was to undo your belt and use it to whack their butt until they cried. What better way to teach somebody not to do something than with the punishment of pain!

These days, most of us have come to the conclusion that beating our child is a bit counterproductive and cruel, and doing so will typically get you thrown in a jail cell. It's just one example of how, every now and then, humankind takes a big leap forward and discovers something that we were doing wrong all along.

One of the most recent big leaps forward in parenting came more than a decade ago from a Stanford psychologist named Carol Dweck, who described a new theory of intelligence around kids who develop a "growth mindset" versus a "fixed mindset." The theory has become so popular and influential that it's not just applicable toward parenting your children, but it's now used with adults and even in corporate settings. It's a big enough deal that it should be one of the main things you focus on as your child develops.

The fixed vs. growth mindset simply deals with two different ways of thinking about where our abilities, talents, and intelligence come from.

The fixed mindset approach is the old-school way of thinking, and it states that everybody is born with innate strengths and weaknesses that are "fixed" and unchangeable. For example, it taught that some people are "just not good at math," and once you discover this, you should avoid math and instead focus on something else that you are naturally good at.

On the other hand, a growth mindset teaches that abilities, talents, and intelligence can be learned and improved upon with enough effort and persistence. It teaches that our success and the things we are able to achieve are largely (although not entirely) within our control, not something fixed that we're either born or not born with. To be clear, having a growth mindset doesn't mean that with enough effort anybody can become a Nobel-prize-winning genius or a professional athlete (and my own experience playing little league baseball proves this), but rather, that people can improve upon themselves if they work at it. As it turns out, adapting this growth mindset of having some control over your own destiny plays a huge role in a person's success and anxiety level over their lifetime. As a result, it's a pretty powerful habit that can make a huge difference in your kid's life (and your own!).

So is it possible to teach our kids to develop a growth mindset, or is it just one of those things that your kid is either born with or not?

That was a trick question! If you're thinking with a growth mindset, then you already know that it's possible to teach your kids to develop a growth mindset. It does take a little work, though. There are lots of different strategies you can use to teach your kids to develop a growth mindset (and to develop a growth mindset of your own along the way). So many strategies, in fact, that I've detailed them out into their own separate pieces of Great Advice. But here's a quick summary:

- Use language that reinforces a growth mindset
- Find appropriate challenges for your kid
- Encourage perseverance
- Celebrate your kid's failures

Teach your child to develop a growth mindset, which will help them realize that they're able to learn almost anything they set their mind to.

"Everything is hard before it is easy."

–Johann Wolfgang von Goethe

DAD'S GREAT ADVICE
FOR
ALL PARENTS #6

USE LANGUAGE THAT REFLECTS A GROWTH MINDSET

Be cognizant of the language you and your child use, and make sure it reinforces a growth mindset every chance you get.

Hopefully, you're already sold on the importance of teaching your child to develop a growth mindset, rather than a fixed mindset. (See *Dad's Great Advice for All Parents #5*, "Teach Your Kids a Growth Mindset," in the bonus section of this book.) But kids aren't just born with a growth mindset, they have to develop it over time. And their parent is just the person to teach them!

The first and easiest step toward teaching your child a growth mindset is to adapt the language you use with your child. When your kid says something that exemplifies a fixed mindset, correct them by reinforcing a growth mindset. You'll be surprised at how often these opportunities come up, and you'll probably be even more surprised about how easy it is to adapt your language once you're focused on noticing it.

In fact, it's so easy that I can sum up the easiest part of adapting your language with one word: "yet."

Just start adding the word "yet" to sentences that relate to your child's abilities. When your kid says something like, "I'm just not good at drawing" (a statement that reflects a fixed mindset that they're just born without drawing skills), you reply, "You're not good at drawing *yet*" (a statement that reflects a growth mindset—they might not be good at drawing now, but once they practice, they'll learn and get better). For extra credit, make that connection even tighter with, "You're not good at drawing *yet*, but you *will* be good at drawing once you practice."

Another simple fix in your language is to expand your definition of swear words that you don't allow in your house. In addition to the big "F-bomb" and the "S-word" and a bunch of other swear words that you probably discourage your kids from using (at least, I hope you do), add a new four-letter word to the list: "can't." When your kid says, "I can't tie my shoes," give them a look like they just dropped an F-bomb and reply, "We do not use that type of language in our house!" Once the look of confusion and amazement disappears from their face, fill them in on the details: "Instead of saying that ugly word, say 'I haven't learned how to tie my shoes yet,' or 'I guess I need to keep practicing before I can tie my shoes.'" (Quick piece of advice: you might want to refrain from referring to "Can't" as "the C-word," as some of us parents learned the hard way that a different C-word has already claimed that title, and it may cause a bit of confusion and embarrassment as a result.)

Once you start to look for it, you'll quickly start to notice other subtle language patterns your kid uses that reflect a fixed mindset, and when you do, you should take the time to correct them. When they say, "It's too hard," you reply, "It's not too hard. It's just hard. But you can learn to do hard things." When they say, "I'm just not a science person," you say, "You're not a science person yet, but you can become a science person if you study." And when they inevitably say, "It's annoying when you correct my language all the time," you say, "Well, once you learn to use a growth mindset, I won't have to!"

Another area of language to focus on is your praise. Lots of parents have the reputation of being "over-praisers" of their kid, praising them for every tiny little accomplishment ("What a great job ripping up that piece of paper!"). Regardless of where you fall on the amount-of-praise spectrum, when you do praise your child, make sure you're praising them in the right way to reinforce a growth mindset. The key is to tie your praise to the effort they made, not the outcome.

For instance, when they solve a tough math problem, don't say, "You're so smart," but rather, "The way you figured that out was so smart." Saying "You're so smart" implies that they only solved the problem because they were born smart, and leaves open the possibility that, with a harder problem, they might not have been born with enough "smartness" to solve it. However, saying "The way you figured that out was so smart" implies that they learned how to figure it out (which was smart), and they can learn how to figure out any other problems that come their way, regardless of how much "smartness" they were born with. The difference between the two might sound to you like a silly distinction that a child wouldn't pick up on, but over time, they most certainly will pick up on it.

Lastly, and perhaps most importantly, no matter how careful you are with your child's language, make sure that you're even more cognizant of the language you use yourself, in the course of your own life. You want to make sure that you're always using language that models a growth mindset, not only because a growth mindset is just as important for you as it is for your child, but also because your kids are always listening to you, even when you think they aren't.

One of the best ways of teaching your child a growth mindset is by focusing on language. Be cognizant of the language you and your child use, and make sure it reinforces a growth mindset every chance you get.

"There's a difference between not knowing and not knowing yet."

–Sheila Tobias

DAD'S GREAT ADVICE
FOR
ALL PARENTS #9

CELEBRATE FAILURE

Failing encourages your child to try new things and take smart risks, so make sure you don't make failure shameful for them.

I'm sorry to have to be the one to tell you this, but I've got some bad news: Your child is going to fail.

Regardless of how careful you and your child are, sooner or later, your child is going to tackle a problem that's simply too big or too difficult for them to accomplish. They're going to fail. And when they fail, it may seem like everything they thought they learned about having a growth mindset, persevering, and developing their abilities was a bunch of crap. But no need to worry! All you need to do is to make sure that you celebrate failure as an integral part of building a growth mindset (because it is!).

I can already hear you: "Hold on there, partner! You're telling me to encourage my child to fail?! That's nuts!"

It is indeed nuts to encourage your kid to fail, so it's a good thing that I'm not telling you to do that. Encourage your child to succeed! But inevitably, when they fall short of their goal, as all of us human beings do from time to time, don't console them. Consoling them teaches your child to abhor failure and be ashamed of failing. And being afraid of failing leads your child to be less likely to try new things and take chances in the future. And being less likely to try new things and take chances in the future causes your child to adopt a fixed mindset and get stuck believing that there's nothing they can do to improve their abilities.

So rather than consoling your kid when they fail and sending them down an awful path, congratulate them, celebrate their failure, and make sure they know why you're celebrating their failure.

And there are lots of reasons to celebrate their failure.

One of the biggest reasons to celebrate their failure is because failure makes us better people, quite literally. Scientists have proven that failure is an important aspect of developing emotional intelligence in children. Kids who are shielded from distress and failure are much more likely to experience depression, anxiety, and hopelessness, and much less likely to develop the important coping mechanisms to help them deal with stress and anxiety.

Teach your child, at a level that's appropriate for their age, how our brains learn. Explain that our brains are a network of microscopic neurons, and as we practice something or try to learn something, the brain sends signals through those neurons. When those signals occur often enough, pathways are created that make it easier in the future for our brain to avoid the wrong signals and recreate the right signals. The same way that exercising your muscles helps those muscles get stronger, making mistakes and failing at things exercises and strengthens your brain. Every time your kid makes a mistake, remind them, "You just made your brain stronger!"

The goal is to normalize failure for kids so they can view failure for what it truly is: an integral step toward achieving success. There are lots of examples of this. For one, when your kid makes a mistake, or fails at something, they've just used the process of elimination to get one step closer to the right way of doing it. "You failed! Great! We now know one more way that doesn't work. Eventually, once we rule out enough of the wrong ways to do it, we'll find the right way."

Another way to normalize failure is to let them watch you fail at something. Pick something you'll have a hard time learning quickly, like skateboarding, juggling, a particularly hard math problem, a TikTok dance, or perhaps even the act of parenting itself. It shouldn't be too hard to find something to fail at! Try that activity in front of your child, and as you obviously fail to immediately learn the activity, celebrate your failure by laughing, smiling, and, most importantly, sharing with your child what you're learning along the way.

Another great way to normalize failure is to highlight all the stories out there of famous people who failed a lot on their way to success. One of the most popular stories celebrating failure is that of Thomas Edison, who tried more than 1,000 different times to create the light bulb before he found the right solution. He then famously said, "I didn't fail 1,000 times. The light bulb was an invention with 1,000 steps." There's also the story of Dr. Spencer Silver, who failed at creating a super strong glue for his company, but instead ended up inventing Post-It Notes for the 3M company, which sells over 50 billion of them each year. And of course, there's the story of the little-known author whose book was rejected by twelve publishers before one brave publisher decided to take a risk on that very special book: *Harry Potter and the Philosopher's Stone.* (I've heard that that author, J. K. Rowling, went on to write a few other pretty darn successful books in that series.)

And don't just celebrate failure. Allow failure to happen. Even though your parent DNA has pre-programmed you to care for your child and protect them from any disappointment, fight that desire and refrain from saving your child from a failure every now and then.

I can already hear you: "You're telling me to let my child fail?! That's nuts!"

Well, letting your kid experience failure is not as nuts as it sounds, especially if you're letting your kid fail early in life when it comes to small things, like forgetting a homework assignment, being late for school, or failing a test.

My good friend Archimedes Clutterbuck got tired of constantly pushing his younger kids to get ready in the morning and leave the house early enough to make it to school on time. So tired, in fact, that on a Sunday evening, he sat his kids down and informed them that, from that moment forward, they were responsible for getting themselves to school on time. They needed to set an alarm for themselves, get themselves ready, and when they were all ready to leave the house, he would walk them to school.

On Monday morning, as promised, Archie quietly waited for his kids to get themselves ready for school, watching patiently as the clock ticked well past the time at which they normally had to leave the house. Spoiler alert: The kids failed miserably and all of them got to school late. The school marked the tardiness on their report cards, and their teachers spoke with each of the kids about being late to class. All in all, it was a failure for the kids—a pretty inconsequential failure in the grand scheme of things, but it seemed VERY consequential to Archie's kids. As a result of that failure, something amazing happened the next day. On Tuesday morning, all of Archie's kids got ready for school super early, and made it to school ten minutes before the bell rang. If that isn't a growth mindset at work, I don't know what is!

So it's OK to let your kid fail occasionally, especially if the consequences of that failure are not enormous. Just make sure that, when they fail, you help them attach a lesson to the failure so they learn something from it.

In fact, you might even take it one step further in some cases and go so far as to reward your child for failing.

There you go again: "Now you're telling me to reward my child for failing?! That's nuts!"

I suppose if that's really what you were actually doing it might be a bit nuts, but luckily, what you're actually doing is rewarding your child not for failing, but for having the courage to try something challenging and risk failure. Particularly when the thing your child failed at required a great deal of courage to attempt, it's perfectly fine to reward them with a gift card, or their favorite dinner, or even some cold, hard cash. Running for class president or trying out for the volleyball team are scary things to attempt for most kids, and having the courage to put themselves out there and risk failure is certainly worthy of praise or a reward. So while you don't want to reward your child for the failure itself, you do want to reward them for trying something outside their comfort zone. In fact, whenever possible, it's always best to try to reward them for their courage to try something before the results of their efforts are revealed. For instance, take your kid out to dinner the same day they try out for the volleyball team—before the results of who made the team are announced. Doing so more clearly ties the reward to the effort, not the result.

One of the interesting things about failure is how closely tied it is to learning. Parents who teach their children that failure is a negative thing to be avoided at all costs are unknowingly teaching their kids to avoid learning new things. If your child tries to do something new and they do it exactly correct on their first try, they've avoided failing at something, but they also haven't learned anything new. They just did something they were already capable of doing. On the other hand, if your child tries something new and fails, that gives them important information about how to improve the next time they try. The failure helps them learn.

Failing encourages your child to try new things and take smart risks, so make sure you don't make failure shameful for them.

"I never lose. I either win or learn."

–Nelson Mandela

DAD'S GREAT ADVICE
FOR
ALL PARENTS #24

DON'T TRY TO BE SUPERPARENT

In order to be a great parent, you just need to be a good parent as often as you can.

There are lots and lots of SuperParents out there. SuperParents make their kids a healthy breakfast, pack a nutritious lunch, get them to school on time, volunteer in the classroom, hold down a full-time job, help with homework, cook a healthy dinner, play a few games, bathe and wash them, read a bedtime story, tuck them in, finish the day with some laundry, and then do it all again the next day. Oh, and of course when conflict does arise, SuperParent handles it calmly, rationally, and logically, without getting upset or screaming at their child. SuperParent is indeed, a super parent.

But just like Superman, SuperParent is a fictional character.

SuperParent doesn't exist in real life. I know this because all parents are human, and humans aren't perfect. That parent you see on social media posting a photo of the amazing homemade apple pie they made for the PTA bake sale? They aren't perfect. That parent you see who shows up to every one of their child's activities? They aren't perfect. That parent you see that handles every one of their child's outbursts calmly, with the skill of a highly trained child psychologist? They aren't perfect either.

Remind yourself that not one parent is getting it all right all the

213

time. Not one. And even though you might see a lot of the successful interactions of many parents, know that they're not always successful. The parent that posts a photo of their apple pie for the PTA bake sale might have bought that pie at the bakery, and then told their kid to lie about it. The parent who shows up to every one of their child's activities might be too busy to spend time with their kid at home. The parent who handles their child's outburst like a pro might totally lose it at home and scream at their kid when nobody else is around to see it.

So don't ever compare yourself to any parents out there who look like SuperParent to you. Don't compare yourself to the SuperParent you meet in person, and especially don't compare yourself to the SuperParent you see on social media. Because none of them are SuperParent. They might look like Clark Kent, but they're really just some random guy with dark hair and thick glasses.

If you're going to compare yourself to a parent, the only parent you should compare yourself to is the parent you were yesterday. If you're an infinitesimally tiny bit better than the parent you were yesterday, it's a win. And if you had what we experts call a "bad parenting day" today and you weren't better today than you were yesterday, don't worry, because you get another chance to try again tomorrow (and the bar is lower now, so tomorrow will almost have to be better!).

In any case, don't try to be SuperParent. As you can tell, there is a lot of Great Advice to be had for parents. Some of that advice is easy to put into practice, and some of it is really, really hard to put into practice. And even though it's all been officially, scientifically certified as Great Advice, you shouldn't try to take all of that Great Advice in at once.

Why? Because it's not easy to do everything all at once. Some might even say it's impossible. So don't try to do it all. In fact, don't even try to do half of it. Try to do one thing. Pick one piece of Great Advice and try to do just that one thing better than you currently do it. And then, once you've mastered that, if you're still up for a challenge, try to do one additional thing.

And remember, it's OK to try to tackle a piece of Great Advice... and fail. Just chalk it up to the fact that being a parent is really hard, offer an apology to your kid or whoever else deserves one, and try again next time.

Most importantly, celebrate the small wins! If you're keeping your child alive, sheltered from the weather, well-hydrated, well-fed (or even just fed), and happy most of the time, you're doing just fine. For a bit of extra credit, try to simply engage and connect with your kid from time to time. And most importantly, celebrate and laugh at all the parenting mistakes and bad decisions you are going to make (and I can promise you there will be a lot of them!), because they give your kid the opportunity to see that not even their own parents are perfect, so they don't have to be perfect either. If you're really on top of your game, maybe your mistake serves as a perfect opportunity to teach your child how to apologize for, fix, and make up for that mistake.

You don't have to be SuperParent to be a great parent. In fact, in order to be a great parent, you just need to be a good parent as often as you can.

"There are no perfect parents, just as there are no perfect children."

–Fred Rogers

HELP AN AUTHOR
(AND ONE HUNDRED MILLION OTHER PEOPLE)

I hope you enjoyed reading *Dad's Great Advice for Parents of Teens* and, more importantly, I hope reading it helps you along your exciting (and treacherous) journey of parenting a teen! If the book was helpful to you, I hope you'll keep reading...

Years ago, I heard one of my all-time favorite pieces of Great Advice from author and speaker (and father of three) Shep Hyken, who insightfully said, "Every interaction you have is an opportunity to make a positive impact on others." Since then, I've made a real effort to put his Great Advice into effect with my children, friends, and everybody I meet, either through offering a piece of Great Advice, telling a "dad joke," or by putting a smile on somebody's face in some other way.

The *Dad's Great Advice* book series began as a way to make a positive impact on just four people. I wrote down all the Great Advice I had collected from parents and experts over the years and printed it in a book written solely for those four people: my children. But word of the book spread, the series quickly grew, and my Great Advice has now had a positive impact on thousands of people all over the world. Still, I wanted to do more.

Eventually, I made it my mission to try to make a positive impact on just 1% of the population. I figure if 100 other people try to do the same, then the whole world will be taken care of. With the world population at just around eight billion people, (and rounding up for inflation) that means I only have to help about 100 million people. No problemo!

The *Dad's Great Advice* book series was born from this mission to help 100 million people. Specifically, my mission to "Have a positive impact on 100 million people with at least one piece of Great Advice that improves each person's life in a meaningful way."

If you've found at least one piece of Great Advice from this book helpful enough to improve your life in a meaningful way, then I'm one additional person closer to achieving that goal. And if so, would you please join me in my mission to help 100 million other people by spreading the word and sharing your favorite piece of Great Advice with one other person you know?

Or if you're busy and that takes too much time, can you simply spend fourteen seconds and one click of a button to leave a rating (from one to five) for this book right now by going to:

greatadvicegroup.com/review6

If you go the extra mile by not only leaving a rating but also leaving a short, one-sentence review of this book, you should know that I read each and every review written, so you have my sincere appreciation!

Thank you for taking the time to read this book. I sincerely hope you found my Great Advice to indeed be great, and I hope you're able to put some of it into action to improve your life and your teen's life in a meaningful way.

Best Regards,

Marc

P.S. If you haven't done so already, make sure you get your free download of *The Top 10 Greatest Great Advice of All Time* here:

greatadvicegroup.com/top10advice6

ABOUT THE AUTHOR

Marc Fienberg spends his free time researching and talking to fellow dads, moms, scientists, psychologists, and experts, trying to learn as much Great Advice as possible to share with the world. He also happens to be an author, movie director, strategy consultant, entrepreneur, owner of The Great Advice Group, husband, father to four teenagers, and all-around nice guy. He has served as a life coach to his kids for almost two decades, and since none of them have been rushed to the emergency room or spent a night in jail yet, it seems like his Great Advice is working. To learn more about him, go to greatadvicegroup.com.

Other Dad's Great Advice Books available at greatadvicegroup.com

Dad's Great Advice for Teens

Dad's Great Advice: Top Ten Greatest Great Advice of All Time

Dad's Great Advice for College Students

Dad's Great Advice for Everyone

Dad's Great Advice for All Parents

Dad's Great Advice About Life Skills for Teens

Made in the USA
Monee, IL
03 April 2023

31253511R00129